CW00664506

33
43
45
47
49
53
54
73
74
76
78
79

The Beauty of Holiness
and the Holiness of Beauty

JOHN SAWARD

THE BEAUTY OF HOLINESS
AND THE
HOLINESS OF BEAUTY

———

Art, Sanctity, and the Truth of Catholicism

IGNATIUS PRESS   SAN FRANCISCO

The Bernard Gilpin Lectures
in Pastoral Theology

The University of Durham
May 1996

Cover art: Fra Angelico, *The San Marco Altarpiece:
Madonna and Child Enthroned with Saints* (detail)
Scala/Art Resource, N.Y.

Cover design by Roxanne Mei Lum

ISBN 0–89870–632–7
Library of Congress catalogue number 97–70815
Printed in the United States of America ∞

Ad honorem
Beatae Mariae Semper Virginis
Deiparae Totae Pulchrae

O worship the Lord in the beauty of holiness!

—PSALM 96(95):9

In the realm of sensible images, the artist keeps his eyes fixed on the thing he is copying. He does not let himself be turned aside or torn away by anything else he can see. . . . So it is with the artists who love beauty in the soul. Their intense and unfailing contemplation of His fragrant and hidden beauty gives them an unerring likeness of God. . . . They do now gawp at the glory stupidly lauded by the mob, but by the imitation of God they distinguish between good and evil. They are divine images of the fragrant Godhead.

—DIONYSIUS THE AREOPAGITE

The Church, which was once the mother of poets no less than of saints, during the last two centuries has relinquished to aliens the chief glories of poetry, if the chief glories of holiness she has preserved for her own. The palm and the laurel, Dominic and Dante, sanctity and song, grew together in her soil: she has retained the palm, but forgone the laurel. Poetry in its widest sense, and when not professedly irreligious, has been too much and too long either misprised or distrusted; too much and too generally the feeling has been that it is at best superfluous, at worst pernicious, most often dangerous. Once poetry was, as she should be, the lesser sister and helpmate of the Church; the minister to the mind, as the Church to the soul. But poetry sinned, poetry fell; and in place of lovingly reclaiming her, Catholicism cast her from the door to follow the feet of her pagan seducer. The separation has been ill for poetry; it has not been well for religion.

—FRANCIS THOMPSON

The only really effective apologia for Christianity comes down to two arguments, namely, the *saints* the Church has produced and the *art* which has grown in her womb. Better witness is borne to the Lord by the splendour of holiness and art which have arisen in the community of believers than by the clever excuses which apologetics has come up with to justify the dark sides which, sadly, are so frequent in the Church's human history. If the Church is to continue to transform and humanize the world, how can she dispense with beauty in her liturgies, that beauty which is so closely linked with love and with the radiance of the Resurrection? No. Christians must not be too easily satisfied. They must make their Church into a place where beauty—and hence truth—is at home. Without this the world will become the first circle of Hell.

—JOSEPH CARDINAL RATZINGER

CONTENTS

FOREWORD

There are three great gateways to God, of goodness, truth, and beauty, yet in the Christian West, they have been sundered by the emergence of first a Protestant and then a secular culture. Neither truth nor goodness now need seem beautiful, and beauty in creation and creature has become, at best, a mere projection of subjective experience, at worst, a worldly temptation and a snare to turn the heart and mind from the eternal.

Yet Satan is no more the author of beauty than of goodness or of truth, for all three come from God—the Father, the Son, and the Spirit, the Trinity in Unity—and have their final harmony in Him. There is a heavenly beauty about the unity belonging to the Trinity in the Christian truths of creation, redemption, and deification, in which the Eternal God who made the world and man first made them good, and then redeemed man from sin and death through His Son, and in that redemption began the restoration of the whole creation to a greater glory. So the divine Son through whom the world was made became very flesh of man to save him, and to make him God, and both creation and man are good in their origin and in their end, and in their beauty reflect their divine original. But man himself, being made in the image of a maker, is himself a maker or re-maker of beauty, a beauty that flows from the Craftsman-Creator and like the divine light in Christ at His Transfiguration shines through the whole creation. Thus beauty is no mere subjective value in the eye of the beholder, nor the delight in the lust of the eye of flesh, but, quite as much as goodness and truth, belongs to an objective reality almost beyond our reason and experience, though we distantly behold its splendour. And so in lowlier measure, the universe in its beauty, as in its truth and goodness, worships and proclaims its celestial origin and end, its alpha and omega, and man is privileged to perceive, and then to re-create in the art through which he offers his author praise and thanksgiving, the reflected and transmuted glory of the God who made him to be His forever.

John Saward's book is a meditation on these themes, arising from a painting by Fra Angelico, who embodied in the spiritual beauty of his life as well as in his work the teaching of the great medieval Dominican and Franciscan scholar-saints and translated that teaching into the lovely images of a Renaissance Catholic culture. Angelico proclaimed the truth and goodness of God anew through the beauty of the images employed in worship, which present Him for that worship in the beauty of holiness both in Himself and in His Incarnation and in the lives and deeds of His saints, above all, in the Virgin Mary, His Mother, the very pinnacle of His creation. No painter realised more completely than Angelico the beauty of the resurrection body before God in the divine liturgy in Paradise. No one else has more adequately portrayed the perfected radiance of the saints before the throne. No one else has made the altarpieces that preside above the Mass so suggestive of the courts of heaven. And in Angelico's pictures, the highest theology and ethics cleanse the senses and the imagination in the loveliness of paint, proclaiming the unity of truth, goodness, and beauty and their power to hallow the mind and heart and to raise them, through the worship of His Body and Blood in the Mass and in the veneration of the saints, to their final end, in the vision of God.

Professor Saward puts Angelico firmly in his setting in that springtime of the spirit, that Florentine Renaissance in which Christian art paid the homage of Christian worship to Christian truth and holiness. But Professor Saward ranges far beyond the artist's time and place to illustrate Angelico's themes with an extraordinary erudition, from the Bible and the Fathers and the Schoolmen to modern poetry. He thereby shows the manner in which one part of the Christian Tradition can illuminate any other and how, in depicting the loveliness of Christ and his creatures, Angelico declares both the timeless truth of their teaching and their holiness of life, from the first Christian century to ours.

Sometimes a thing is more easily defined by its negation. Readers may be offended by Professor Saward's discussion of the Reformation. Its treatment of Durham Cathedral is their refutation, as is the subsequent history of Protestant art. Protestantism secularised the image by declaring it idolatrous. The vacuum created by the Enlightenment's destruction of a Catholic culture has been filled by a secular culture whose images have become increasingly depraved and whose central icons, like the screaming popes of Francis Bacon and the pop singer Madonna, are parodies of the Catholicism they seek both to exploit and to destroy. The poverty of so much modern Catholic art, and its separation from theological study and holiness of life, together speak of a sickness at the heart of our Western culture. Only through the recovery of Angelico's holistic vision—in which eye as well as ear finds delight in divine truth, which is known not in pride, but in humility, on our knees in worship—will we recapture Angelico's realisation, in images filled with light from heaven, of the radiance of God's glory.

Sheridan Gilley
University of Durham

ACKNOWLEDGEMENTS

These acknowledgements are a tale of two cities. *The Beauty of Holiness and the Holiness of Beauty* was conceived in Philadelphia, at St Charles Borromeo Seminary, where it was first presented in the form of a seminar in the Summer School of the Religious Studies Division. I thank my students for their enthusiasm and Mrs Lorena Boylan and her colleagues in the library for their unfailing courtesy and helpfulness.

Conceived in Philadelphia as a seminar, the book was born in Durham as a series of lectures. I am deeply grateful to the Department of Theology of the University of Durham for honouring me with an invitation to deliver the Bernard Gilpin Lectures in Pastoral Theology in May 1996. In particular, I must thank my friends and former colleagues Dr Sheridan Gilley and Dr Robert Hayward for their gracious hospitality and generous encouragement. It was a glorious privilege to be able to speak about the beauty of Christ and His saints within sight of the noble church built to honour St Cuthbert.

I must also express my heartfelt gratitude to my wife and three daughters for a thousand and one contributions to this book. Among other things, I argue here that the family is the foundation of artistic culture, as it is also of society. For my part, I know that my family is the rock upon which my life rests. In a special way, I want to thank my daughter Helena for her many insights and perceptions. Some of these she shared with me as together we explored the beauty and holiness of Rome.

I dedicate the book to the memory of my father, G. J. 'Johnnie' Saward, who loved the great art of Christian culture and taught me to love it, too, when I was a little boy. I can still feel the squeeze of his hand as we walked round the National Gallery in London, and I pray for his soul in the words of the Byzantine liturgy: 'To him who has departed, mercifully grant thine ineffable glory, O Lord, and thine inexpressible blessedness in the mansions of the Saints, where fair is the voice of those who keep high festival. Reward him with the life that knows no suffering, O thou who alone lovest mankind!'

John Saward

The Assumption of Our Lady
15 August 1996
St Charles Borromeo Seminary

ABBREVIATIONS

AAS   *Acta apostolicae sedis* (Rome, 1909–).

CCC   *Catechism of the Catholic Church.*

CCSL   *Corpus christianorum: series latina* (Turnholti, 1953–).

DS   H. Denzinger and A. Schönmetzer, *Enchiridion symbo-lorum, definitionum et declarationum de rebus fidei et morum,* 36th ed. (Rome, 1976).

ET   English translation.

GL   Hans Urs von Balthasar, *The Glory of the Lord: A Theological Aesthetics* (Edinburgh, 1982–1991) (ET of *Herrlichkeit*).

H   Hans Urs von Balthasar, *Herrlichkeit: Eine theologische Ästhetik* (Einsiedeln, 1961–1969).

Mansi   J. D. Mansi, *Sacrorum conciliorum nova et amplissima collectio* (Florence, 1759–1798).

PG   J. P. Migne, *Patrologia graeca* (Paris, 1857–1866).

PL   J. P. Migne, *Patrologia latina* (Paris, 1844–1902).

SC   *Sources chrétiennes* (Paris, 1940–).

Sent.   *Scriptum super libros Sententiarum.*

ST   *Summa theologiae.*

I

Ipse Est Corona Sanctorum

THE BEAUTY OF CHRIST
AND HIS SAINTS

Christ in His heavenly beauty does not shine alone. There is no splendid isolation in His Godhead, for He is Light from Light, the consubstantial Son and Splendour of the Father, living and reigning with Him in the unity of the Holy Spirit. And the glory of His manhood is not a private radiance, for He is the Light of the World, the Bridegroom who beautifies the Bride, the Lamb who is the lamp of a lustrous city. The brightness of Christ's pierced and risen flesh is incomparable but not incommunicable. He is 'beautiful above the sons of men', and yet 'grace is poured abroad in [His] lips' (Ps 44:3). On His right stands the Queen (Ps 44:10), His Virgin Mother, clothed body and soul in His glory, and around her is her court, the numberless multitude made brilliant in His blood. 'Ipse est corona sanctorum', He is the crown of all the saints, '*Ipse*, the only one, Christ, King, Head'.[1]

As a boy Bernard Gilpin[2] saw this dogmatic truth—the

[1] Gerard Manley Hopkins, 'The Wreck of the Deutschland', st. 28, in *The Poetical Works of Gerard Manley Hopkins*, ed. N. H. Mackenzie (Oxford, 1990), 126. 'Ipse est corona sanctorum' is from the Invitatory antiphon for Matins in the old Dominican Breviary.

[2] Bernard Gilpin was born in Westmoreland in 1517 and educated at Queen's College, Oxford, where he absorbed the writings and ideas of

truth of the Communion of Saints—set forth in iconic beauty
in every church of the realm: in altarpieces and wall paintings,
in shrines and portals, in stone and in glass. From these images,
a Catholic lad of the 1520s would learn that, in the Virgin's
womb, the Father's invisible Word had been made visible flesh
and that, on the altar, He with His Sacrifice was truly present,
joining earthly to heavenly Church. The churches of Gilpin's
North Country had long been blessed with images of Christ
and His saints. St Bede reports that St Benet Biscop brought
back holy pictures from Rome to fill the vaults and walls of St
Peter's, Wearmouth. The holy images were set up, he says,

> so that all who entered the church, even the unlettered, should
> look upon the ever lovely face of Christ and His saints, albeit in
> a picture; or with more vigilant mind might remember the
> grace of the Lord's Incarnation; or, with the danger of the Last
> Judgement, as it were, before their eyes, might remember more
> rigorously to examine themselves.[3]

Of all the churches of medieval England, none bore witness
to the beauty of Christ and His saints more splendidly than
Gilpin's great-uncle's church, the monastic Cathedral of Durham.[4] As its first chronicler, Simeon of Durham (c. 1060–1130),

---

Erasmus. He was later elected one of the first Students of the reconstituted
Christ Church. He seems at first not to have approved of the change in religion and in 1552 preached pointedly on sacrilege in the presence of Edward
VI. However, he came to accept the Elizabethan Settlement and made a name
for himself as the 'Apostle of the North'. He died in 1583. There is no twentieth-century biography. See the article by G. G. Perry in the *Dictionary of
National Biography*, vol. 21 (1890), 378–80.

[3] St Bede the Venerable, *Vita Sanctorum Abbatum*, lib. 1; PL 94, 718A.

[4] Gilpin's great-uncle was Cuthbert Tunstall (1474–1559), Bishop of Durham from 1530. Under Henry VIII, he first opposed but later came to accept
the Royal Supremacy. In the reign of Edward VI, his resistance to the new
religion became more bravely outspoken. He voted against the abolition of
the chantries and of priestly celibacy. Under house arrest in London in 1551
he wrote his treatise *De Veritate Corporis et Sanguinis Domini Nostri Jesu Christi*

says, this 'holy church' owes its very origin to the saints, for 'to the praise of God, it preserves . . . with inviolate care those most sacred relics, worthy of all veneration, the incorrupt body of the most holy father, Cuthbert, and the most adorable head of the king and martyr, Oswald.'[5] Not only in the shrine of St Cuthbert but throughout the cathedral, the Durham Catholic caught signs of a welcoming, open Heaven: 'Jerusalem, my happy home,/ When shall I come to thee?/ When shall my sorrows have an end/ Thy joys when shall I see?'[6] The Neville Screen housed over one hundred richly gilded and painted statues. In the centre was the Virgin Mother of God with her Holy Child, flanked on either side by St Cuthbert and St Oswald. In these images that portrayed Paradise, as in the chantries that pointed to Purgatory, the man of faith was taught that there is one Mystical Body of Christ, one Christendom in divers states (militant, expectant, and triumphant), and that among all Christ's members, by the working of the Holy Spirit, there is communion, an exchange of spiritual goods. To the monks and townsfolk of Durham, St Cuthbert was a friend and father, a close companion and benefactor. Through his incessant prayers in Heaven and his incorrupt body on earth, he brought men the strength and healing of Christ.

---

in Eucharistia (Paris, 1554). Having been restored to his bishopric by Queen Mary, he incurred the displeasure of Elizabeth. He refused to take the Oath of Supremacy and to consecrate Matthew Parker as Archbishop of Canterbury. He was deprived of his see and handed over to Parker as a prisoner in Lambeth Palace. He died some weeks later. Bishop Tunstall is one of eleven confessor-bishops who died in prison for the faith. See C. Sturge, *Cuthbert Tunstall* (New York, 1938).

[5] Simeon of Durham, *Historia Ecclesiae Dunelmensis*, chap. 1; *Opera omnia*, ed. T. Arnold, vol. 1 (Rolls Series, 1882), 1.

[6] This is the first stanza of an anonymous poem, of recusant provenance, apparently first printed in 1601 in *The Song of Mary the Mother of Christ* (see L. I. Guiney, *Recusant Poets, with a Selection from Their Work* [London and New York, 1938], 278).

The twofold beauty that graced the Durham of Gilpin's boy-hood, the beauty stripped from the Durham of Gilpin's man-hood, is the subject of these Gilpin lectures: the beautiful holiness of the Church's saints and the holy beauty of the Church's art. It will be an essay at once dogmatic and pastoral. Dogmatically, I shall try to show how, through holy persons and hallowed art, the splendour of Christ the Truth shines upon the human mind. Pas-torally, I hope to prove that, through the attractive loveliness of sanctity and iconography, the Good Shepherd can draw lost sheep to the fold and keep them safe within. These are not the only lessons by which Christ the Teacher enlightens us (His truth is infallibly proclaimed by the Magisterium of His Church), nor are they the only visible signs by which Christ the Priest and Pastor guides us (His seven Sacraments confer a gift greater than all art). However, these two privileged parts of the Church's Tradition are seldom considered in their dogmatic, apologetical, and pastoral power, and to this task I now commit myself.

My subject is the saints and art, or rather it is the transcendent beauty of the Triune God revealed in the incarnate Word, the Lord Jesus Christ, a beauty that both saintly lives and sacred arts in their different ways radiate. My intentions are threefold. First, taking my inspiration from Hans Urs von Balthasar, I want to expound a 'theological aesthetic' of Christian sanctity and art. Like Balthasar, my interest is in a 'theological aesthetic', not an 'aesthetic theology'.[7] I am not trying to reduce the Creed to subjective impressions of beauty, to pretty poetry and suggestive symbols, but to perceive—through holy men and holy images—the objective glory of divinely revealed truth.[8]

---

[7] H 1, 74ff.; GL 1, 79ff.

[8] Something similar was attempted by Chateaubriand in the early years of the nineteenth century, only a few years after revolutionary Terror had en-gulfed the Church in France. In his *Génie du christianisme* he extols the 'Beau-ties of the Christian Religion', the splendour of its doctrine, and the magnificence of its faith-inspired art. Noble though it is, Chateaubriand's

There is a paradox in this project. Sensible beauty draws the eyes and the heart. It captures our attention and evokes our wonder. The spiritual beauty of the saints has similar effects. It inspires admiration. It provokes others to take the same path, to respond to Christ's call to be perfect as the heavenly Father is perfect. This has been evident, throughout the history of the Church, in the magnetic influence of such men and women as St Aidan and St Cuthbert, St Francis and St Dominic, St Catherine of Siena and St Teresa of Avila. But there is the rub. The saints strive to lead men to Christ, not to themselves. The Saviour, not self, is their centre. They insist with King David: 'Not to us, O Lord, not to us, but to thy name give glory' (Ps 113:9). Like the Apostles at Lystra, the saints tear their garments when they receive the flattery of men (cf. Acts 14:13). They resist men's veneration in order to combat Satan's temptation: the trap of spiritual pride. St Catherine accepts the pains of Christ's wounds in her body but asks for their marks to be hidden. Some of the saints even try to make themselves repellent. The holy fools of Byzantium live as beggars and half-wits, while St Philip Neri shaves off half his beard and goes to the altar in white boots.[9] And yet it is this very humility, their pointing to Christ rather than themselves, that draws men to the saints.

---

undertaking is fatally flawed. As Balthasar has shown, he sets his horizon of beauty too low. He measures the beauty of Divine Revelation by 'this-worldly, human, and cultural beauty', which is 'appropriate for the effects of Christianity, but not valid for the essence of Christianity itself' (H 1, 88; GL 1, 94). Moreover, his attack on Voltairean rationalism sometimes looks like a retreat into subjectivism. For example, when he announces that, in the *Génie*, he will avoid 'abstract ideas' (for example, the traditional proofs of the existence of God) and employ instead 'poetic reasons and reasons of sentiment' (*Oeuvres complètes*, vol. 14 [Paris, 1836], 139), he sounds suspiciously like the fastidious Anglican Modernists, whose 'suave Politeness', as Ronald Knox oberved in *Absolute and Abitofhell*, 'tempering bigot Zeal,/ Corrected "I believe" to "One does feel"' (*Essays in Satire* [London, 1928], 85).

[9] See my book *Perfect Fools: Folly for Christ's Sake in Catholic and Orthodox Spirituality* (Oxford, 1980), 19ff., 97ff.

There is nothing less winning than self-centred cupidity, nothing more engaging than self-giving charity. The Christ-centred saints are radiant with His likeness. 'It is no longer I who live, but Christ who lives in me' (Gal 2:20). They are transparent to Jesus. They let us see and hear Him. That is why all of the saints are teachers, theologians indeed, an unlettered peasant like St Joan of Arc as well as a learned patrician like St Basil the Great.[10] 'He who loves', says St John, 'is born of God and knows God' (1 Jn 4:7). The saints love God, and they know Him, and from their loving knowledge, they teach us.

The second intention of this book is to enliven dogmatic and pastoral theology with an infusion of hagiography and iconography. Hans Urs von Balthasar regarded the separation of theology from sanctity as the most tragic divorce in the history of the Church. In an essay written over forty years ago, he pointed out that, since the golden age of Scholasticism, the Church has found few theologians in whom she recognizes heroic virtue.[11] By contrast, in the Patristic centuries and during the Middle Ages (up to and including the great Schoolmen), the great theologians were saints: they practised what they preached and preached what they practised. Sacred learning coincided with saintly living. The sanctity of the theologians gave the People of God a great confidence in their teaching. Their faith was vibrantly alive with charity, and their understanding of faith perfected by the Gifts of the Holy Spirit. They spoke with authority of the God whom they loved above all else.

Whenever the Patristic and medieval unity is lost, theology turns into ideology, and spirituality becomes psychology. In the heresy of Modernism, we find a vivid example of this disinte-

---

[10] See François-Marie Léthel, O.C.D., *Connaître l'amour du Christ qui surpasse toute connaissance: La Théologie des saints* (Venasque, 1989), 5ff.

[11] 'Theologie und Heiligkeit', *Wort und Wahrheit* 3 (1948): 881f. (reprinted in *Verbum Caro*, vol. 1 of *Skizzen zur Theologie* [Einsiedeln, 1960]; ET, *The Word Made Flesh*, vol. 1 of *Explorations in Theology* [San Francisco, 1989], 181ff.).

gration: a vague 'mysticism', a cult of subjective experience, displaces the objective truth of Divine Revelation, leaving theology the degrading task of applauding worldly wisdom. Something similar happens when theology is cut off from iconography. Without the holy images, we are in danger of forgetting the face and thus the flesh of the Son of God. The mysteries of the life of Jesus fade from our minds. In the eighth and ninth and sixteenth centuries, and again in our own time, Iconoclasm always tends towards Docetism. Robbed of the beauty of sacred art, the Christian can become blind to the beauty of Divine Revelation. And that is disastrous, for, when sundered from beauty, truth becomes a correctness without splendour and goodness a value of no delight. As Balthasar says:

> Our situation shows that beauty demands for herself at least as much courage and decision as do truth and goodness, and she will not allow herself to be separated and banned from her two sisters without taking them along with herself in an act of mysterious vengeance. We can be sure that whoever sneers at her name as if she were the ornament of a bourgeois past—whether he admits it or not—can no longer pray and soon will no longer be able to love.[12]

Thirdly, I want to repeat Our Lord's call to holiness: 'Be perfect as your heavenly Father is perfect' (Mt 5:48). As the Fathers of the Second Vatican Council said, the universal call to sanctity is 'a fundamental requirement arising from the mystery of the Church'.[13] She is the chosen Vine whose branches live and grow with the very sap of Christ, the Mystical Body whose limbs receive supernatural life from the Head, the Bride of Jesus, who

---

[12] H 1, 16; GL 1, 18. In his later work *Theologik*, Balthasar writes: 'Truth, goodness, and beauty are transcendental attributes of being, so much so that they can only be understood in one another and through one another. Together they prove the inexhaustible depth and overflowing richness of being' (*Wahrheit der Welt*, vol. 1 of *Theologik* [Einsiedeln, 1985], 255).

[13] *Lumen Gentium*, no. 42.

gave Himself up on the Cross for her sanctification. What the Church is corporately, her members must personally be. Those who in her Sacraments are given the Christ-life of grace must actually live it. Christians are called to become what they are by their Baptism: children of the Father, members of the Son, temples of the Holy Spirit, partakers of the life of the Blessed Trinity.

This book will be a theological meditation on one work of Christian art: the altarpiece from the Convent of San Marco in Florence, painted by Fra Angelico in the late 1430s.[14] Giorgio Vasari, the biographer of the Italian Renaissance, described it as 'especially beautiful and marvellous',[15] while Ruskin was convinced that Angelico 'intended it to be his masterpiece'.[16] In the holy beauty of this painting, the beautiful holiness of Paradise sheds its rays upon earth. It is meant to move men towards sanctity. This Madonna, says Vasari, 'inspires devotion in the beholder by her simplicity, and the saints who stand around her do likewise.'[17] It is itself the work of a saint, for Fra Angelico is Brother John of Fiesole of the Order of Preachers, long venerated by his brethren and in 1983 officially granted a liturgical cult by Pope John Paul II together with the title 'Blessed'.[18]

---

[14] My understanding of Fra Angelico in general, and of this painting in particular, is indebted to Georges Didi-Huberman, *Fra Angelico: Dissemblance and Figuration* (Chicago and London, 1995), and William Hood, *Fra Angelico at San Marco* (London, 1993).

[15] Giorgio Vasari, *Le vite de'più eccellenti pittori, scultori ed architettori*, vol. 2 of *Opere*, new ed. (Florence, 1906), 504.

[16] 'The Schools of Art in Florence', in *The Works of Ruskin*, vol. 23 (London, 1906), 262.

[17] Vasari, *Vite*, 508. Having been scrubbed with carbolic soap in the last century, the painting no longer glows with its original brightness. Its *claritas* is now a memory.

[18] This was done through a *motu proprio* that begins with the famous words of Fra Angelico: 'Qui res Christi gerit, oportet Christo semper adhaereat', the one who does the work of Christ must always cling to Him (AAS 75 [1983], 796–99).

In each chapter of this book, I am going to take Angelico's icon of Christ and the saints as a theological source, a *locus theologicus*. I shall try to unfold its 'theological aesthetic' with the aid of Angelico's own sources: the sacred authors of Scripture, the Fathers and Doctors of the Church, and the theologians of the Dominican Order, above all St Thomas Aquinas.

1. Fra Angelico: The Artist-Saint

The Art of Holy Living

Brother John of Fiesole was the simplest of men, kindly and modest, a friend of the poor, who 'sought no dignity and had no care but to escape Hell and to get closer to Paradise'. He believed that 'the one who does the work of Christ must always cling to Christ.'[19] He never took up his brush without first kneeling to pray. He wept as he painted the Crucified.

Sanctity alone does not make a man a great painter, but when a great painter is also a saint, when he allows the Holy Spirit to supernaturalise the natural genius with which he has been blessed, then his art achieves a matchless purity.[20] St Thomas Aquinas defines as 'connatural' that knowledge which a man has of something by sharing in it.[21] The honest man has an immeasurably deeper knowledge of honesty than a dishonest professor of moral theology. Fra Angelico depicts sanctity with the authority of connatural knowledge. He can depict loving devotion to Christ's Passion, humility, purity, and compassion for the poor with stunning authenticity because his own life radiates all these beautiful virtues. We are not surprised by Vasari's judgment:

[19] Vasari, *Vite*, 520.
[20] See the discussion of art and sanctity below, 84ff.
[21] St Thomas discusses connatural knowledge in ST 2a2ae 45, 2.

'The saints he painted have more the air and likeness of saints than those of anyone else.'[22]

Fra Angelico was born at the end of the fourteenth century in the Mugello valley in Tuscany and baptized Guido. He entered the novitiate of the Dominicans of the Strict Observance at the convent of San Domenico in Fiesole, taking the name John, and in about 1427 he was ordained to the priesthood. Nine years later, the reformed Dominicans took possession of the convent of San Marco in Florence and soon began to restore the buildings. With the financial backing of the de Medici brothers, Cosimo and Lorenzo, they rebuilt the former church of the Sylvestrine order. Fra Angelico was commissioned to paint a high altarpiece and to decorate the corridors and cells with frescoes. It was a priceless gift for his brethren: he enabled them to have contemplative contact with the mysteries of the life of Jesus at every moment of their day. Angelico practised his art in many other places—Cortona, Orvieto, and above all Rome, where he served Popes Eugenius IV and Nicholas V. Impressed as much by the man and friar as by the artist, Pope Nicholas offered Angelico the archbishopric of Florence, but he 'begged to be excused, since he did not feel capable of ruling men'. Instead he suggested his confrère and patron, St Antoninus: 'a friend of the poor', said Angelico, 'and someone who feared God'.[23] Blessed John, the 'Angelic Friar', died in Rome in February 1455 and is buried in the Church of Santa Maria sopra Minerva, just a few feet away from the tomb of St Catherine of Siena. One of the inscriptions on his grave calls him 'venerable', 'true little servant of the Lord'.

The San Marco altarpiece was painted at a turning point in the history of the West. Gothic art—dogmatic, contemplative, still close in spirit, despite its greater affectivity and naturalism, to the icons of Byzantium—is giving way to the more sensuous

[22] Vasari, *Vite*, 520.
[23] Ibid., 517.

forms of the Renaissance. The Latin and Greek Churches are in dialogue at the reunion Council of Florence. From February 1439, while Fra Angelico paints the saints in San Marco, not far away in the same city his Dominican colleagues are discussing the *Filioque* with Mark Eugenicus and Bessarion. The scent of a second spring is in the air. The Western Great Schism has recently been healed. There are new moves afoot to promote both the beauty of holiness and the holiness of beauty. The Church's buildings are being refurbished in splendour, while her members are being called to reclothe themselves in sanctity.

The renewal of the Church in Angelico's lifetime was due in part to the earthly efforts and heavenly intercession of a woman, St Catherine of Siena, who had died at the age of thirty-three more than fifty years before. She urged the Pope ('dear *Babbo*') to return to Rome and to a braver fidelity to *Gesù dolce*. Writing to a 'great prelate', this dyer's daughter says that the Church's pastors should hunger, not for the comfort of the world's pastures, but, like the Lamb-Shepherd Himself, for the salvation of the flock alone. She offers no programme but the Cross: 'Hide yourself in the wounds of Christ Crucified', she exhorts him, 'bathe in the Blood of Christ Crucified.' Then she adds, talking, as Sigrid Undset says of the saint's dealings with the Popes, 'like an unhappy little girl with her father': 'Forgive me my presumption!' [24]

St Catherine's mission was continued in the Order of Preachers by her spiritual sons. She and her confessor, Blessed Raymond of Capua, inspired Blessed John Dominic Banchini (c. 1355–1419) to call the Order to a more radical fidelity to its Constitutions.[25] The Friars of the Strict Dominican Observance

---

[24] *Lettera* 16, in *Lettere scelte di Santa Caterina da Siena*, 3d ed. (Siena, 1984), 50. See S. Undset, *Catherine of Siena* (New York, 1954), 170.

[25] See the *Acta Sanctorum*, June, vol. 2 (Antwerp, 1698), 394–418, especially the eulogy by St Antoninus, 396f.; and A. Peter, *Studien über den Kardinal Johannes Dominici* (Freiburg, 1911).

were to rededicate themselves to preaching, 'not in the persuasive words of human wisdom, but in showing of the Spirit and
power' (1 Cor 2:4).[26] The Divine Office, including the Night
Office, was to be celebrated without haste or short-cuts. Gospel
poverty was to be practised without accommodations.[27]

John Dominic is an enigma. At first sight he looks like the
typical man of his age, a 'Renaissance man', with broad interests
and large sympathies. He wrote works of spiritual theology, Biblical exegesis, history, education, and poetry.[28] He was a faithful
son of St Thomas, yet also a grateful student of St Bernard and
St Bonaventure.[29] However, when we try to observe him more
closely, he steps into the light as boldly countercultural. He refused to be swept away by the new humanism and insisted that
the pagan classics should be read selectively, with faith-directed
discernment.[30] Unlike the fashionable preachers, he did not fill
out his sermons with quotations from the pagan poets and philosophers but instead broke open the Scriptures 'with new and
wonderful expositions'.[31] After his death, the spiritual leadership
of the Strict Dominican Observance passed to Antoninus
Pierozzi, who, as we have seen, probably became Archbishop of
Florence through the mediation of Fra Angelico. St Antoninus
was not only a zealous reforming pastor but also a wise pastoral
theologian. His *Summa Theologica* went through twenty editions
and, together with the *Summa Confessionis*, shaped much of the
confessional practice of the next hundred years. As a theologian

[26] Cf. *Acta Sanctorum*, 404f.

[27] John himself did not even possess 'books to read or a Bible to preach
from' (St Antoninus in the *Acta Sanctorum*, 396f.).

[28] He is the author of one of the loveliest religious poems of the fourteenth
century, the *Ricordi dell'infanzia di Gesù*, a dialogue with 'Maria dolce' about
her Baby, 'Cristo mio Dio' (see O. Targioni-Tozzetti, *Antologia della poesia
italiana*, new ed. [Leghorn, 1923], 138).

[29] Cf. R.-L. Oechslin, 'B. Jean Dominici', *Dictionnaire de spiritualité* 8:478.

[30] See his *Lucula noctis*, written in 1406 against Coluccio Salutati, ed. E.
Hunt (Notre Dame, 1940).

[31] St Antoninus, *Acta Sanctorum*, 396f.

and Biblical exegete, he is described by Henri de Lubac as a 'fervent disciple of St Thomas'.[32] It was he who founded the Convent of San Marco and encouraged the work of his confrere, the Angelic Friar from Fiesole.

These, then, were the times in which Fra Angelico painted his masterpiece, and these the men who shaped his mind.

The Masterpiece

The new altar in the church of San Marco, Florence, was dedicated to SS. Cosmas and Damian, the patron saints of the community's benefactor, Cosimo de Medici. The predella of the altar contained a sequence of nine paintings depicting scenes from the life of the martyrs. The saints in the altarpiece are all patrons: St John the Evangelist (for John of Fiesole himself), St Mark (patron of the convent), St Lawrence (for Lorenzo de Medici), St Dominic (founder of the Order of Preachers), St Peter Martyr (Dominican protomartyr), St Francis (spiritual father of every mendicant).

The painting displays the fellowship of the angels and saints with each other and with us. The perspective of the slanting floor gives an impression of depth, enhanced by the altar crucifix painted in the vertical plane. Fra Angelico wants to show Heaven as open to earth. The drapes are pulled back. We can step right in. The Madonna is showing us the blessed Fruit of her womb. St Mark confers with St John; Dominic is turned towards Francis. An exchange is going on within Heaven and between Heaven and earth. Art historians call this kind of painting a *sacra conversazione*. We may call it the *Communio Sanctorum*. St Damian has his back to us and is lost in contemplation. St Cosmas is turned towards us, pointing with his right hand towards Our Lord and Our Lady. His face is marked by deep

[32] H. de Lubac, *Exégèse médiévale: Les quatre sens de l'écriture*, vol. 2/2 (Paris, 1964), 302.

emotion. He is inviting us, pleading with us, to take the way of holiness, to take up our cross and follow the Lord Jesus.

The choir chapel of San Marco was dedicated, in the presence of Pope Eugenius IV, on the feast of the Epiphany 1443. The altarpiece suggests a verse from the Gospel of the day: 'Going into the house, they saw the Child with Mary His Mother, and they fell down and worshipped Him' (Mt 2:10f.), a text for which one of Angelico's theological sources, St Albert the Great, provides the following gloss:

> The house that the soul enters, led by the star (that is, grace), is the house of eternal glory. There is found Jesus, not lying in abjection in the manger, but seated in honour on His kingly throne. . . . Sitting at the right of her Son is the undefiled Virgin Mary. . . . Ask, therefore, the Lord, to make us wise, faithful, humble, merciful kings, so that, after this life, by the leading of the star, that is, by God's grace, we may come to happiness in the presence of Jesus and His Mother.[33]

The altarpiece preaches no other message.

2. The Sources of Angelico's Theological Aesthetic

The Angels

Immediately around her throne, Our Lady is assisted by eight angels. They have a human appearance, the semblance of a human body, for that is how they show themselves to the saints, and that is why these pure spirits can be represented in art.[34] The angels assist Mary, the Queen of Angels, but they also assist John, the Angelic Friar. From Dionysius the Areopagite and St Thomas, and indeed from the whole Tradition, Angelico learned

[33] *Sermo 12 in Epiphania Domini*, no. 3; *Beati Alberti Magni opera omnia*, ed. A. Borgnet, vol. 13 (Paris, 1891), 63.

[34] Cf. St Thomas, ST 1a 51, 2.

that the angels illuminate the mind of man.[35] Light cascades from the Trinitarian Godhead through the celestial hierarchies of the angels. St Thomas tells us that the angels cannot act directly upon the intellect, but they can touch the senses and the imagination.[36] The holy angels plant good thoughts in our minds by clothing them in images of virtue, while the fallen angels entice us towards evil through images of vice. The saint-artist is one who lets his imagination be purified and enriched by the icons given him by the angels.

Angelico's angels are beautiful. This is fitting, because, according to St Thomas Aquinas, in their nature, the angels have the highest beauty after God.[37] In what they are and what they do, in their relations to each other and to man in the visible world, the angels are magnificent. Their nature has the beauty of pure spirituality.[38] They know and will with a wonderful swiftness and immediacy.[39] Their number, surpassing all material multitude, dazzles man's mind.[40] The angels exist and function in a diversity beyond anything in the material world. Each angel differs in species from his fellows,[41] and all are united in a glorious array of choirs and hierarchies.[42]

A flight of eight angels sings to Heaven's sweet Queen. This serving and praising posture is instructive. Despite the supreme beauty of their natures, the angels are not the greatest after God. The Virgin Mother of God is more honourable than the Cherubim and incomparably more glorious than the Seraphim. No high angel is as close to the Trinity as the humble Handmaid of the Lord. When Gabriel says, 'The Lord is with thee', he makes

[35] Ibid., III, I.
[36] Ibid., III, 3 and 4; 1a2ae 80, 2.
[37] Cf. 2 Sent., d. 9, q. 1, a. 5, sed contra 2.
[38] Cf. ST 1a 50, 1.
[39] Ibid., qq. 54–60.
[40] Ibid., 50, 3.
[41] Ibid., 50, 4.
[42] Ibid., q. 108.

The San Marco Altarpiece: *Madonna and Child Enthroned with Angels and Ss. Cosmas and Damian, Laurence, John the Evangelist, Mark, Dominic, Francis and Peter Martyr.*

a genuflection: 'I bow to thee because thou art more familiar with God than I am': with the Father, because His Son is also hers; with the Son, because He is in her womb; and with the Holy Spirit, because He dwells in her as in a temple.[43]

The Devil and his demons are angels who were created good and beautiful by God but who fell into Hell because they fell in love with their own beauty. According to St Thomas, they did not sin 'through the flesh, which they do not have, nor through the sensible things of this world, which they do not need, but by the beauty of their nature'.[44] Through the Prophet, God says to Lucifer: 'Thou hast lost thy wisdom in thy beauty' (Ezek 28:17). St Bonaventure unfolds the argument:

> The angel was created good by God, but not supremely good: he was to be perfected by the movement of his affection towards the highest good. Having free will, Lucifer was able to choose either the Supreme Good or his own private good. The sight of his own beauty and eminence having made him fall in love with himself and his private good, he presumed upon the lofty state already his to aspire to an excellence that he had not yet attained. . . . Since all this was the disorderly effect of a pride-infected will, the fallen angel perverted everything to feed his pride, expecting men to revere and adore him as if he were God. That is why he works all things wickedly.[45]

The sin of Satan is the sin of Narcissus. All diabolical wickedness has at its root a perverted aesthetic. The Devil can and does abuse beauty in order to entice men into the worship of self and the rejection of God. He incites to lust through the beauty of the body, or to pride through the beauty of the mind. More subtly, he tries to sever the beauty of Christian art from the truth of the dogmatic creed and the goodness of the moral virtues. As

---

[43] Cf. St Thomas Aquinas, *In salutationem angelicam*, no. 1.

[44] *De malo* 16, 3, ad 13.

[45] *Breviloquium* 2, 7; *Sancti Bonaventurae opera omnia*, vol. 5 (Quaracchi, 1891), 225.

Theodor Haecker said, writing from Germany at the beginning of the Second World War:

> In this world, nothing is apparently more helpless and power-less than beauty. In the visible order, nothing is more vulner-able, and so nothing falls more easily into the clutches of the Evil Spirit than beauty. There is no demonic truth, there is no demonic goodness, but there really does seem to be a demonic beauty.[46]

Evil itself is not beautiful, for it is the privation of the good (and therefore of the beautiful). However, the Evil Spirit, the fallen angelic creature, can exploit the charm of the beautiful (wheth-er of the body or of the soul, of art or of science) in order to seduce men into rebellion against God.[47] The Devil strives to rob beauty of its transparency, so that a man sees the beauty of the body but not of the mind, is fascinated more by the interest of an idea than by the splendour of the truth, delights in the artistry of the image but is blind to the sanctity of the person imaged.[48] Every worship of beauty that thus falls short of its full depth becomes idolatry.

There is only one protection against the self-serving aesthe-ticism of the Devil: to imitate the good angels by serving the self-emptying Son of God, the infant of the Virgin. The pseudo-beauty of falsehood and evil swears, '*Non serviam*', I will not serve a God so humble. The beauty of truth and goodness prays, 'Be it done unto me according to thy word. . . . Let God be-come a child within me.'[49] The Blessed Virgin Mary, all-holy

---

[46] Theodor Haecker, *Schönheit: Ein Versuch* (Leipzig, 1940), 78.

[47] 'Evil is not beautiful, but the Spirit of Evil exploits beauty, the beauty that does not belong to him, still less is made by him' (ibid., 79).

[48] Ibid., 91.

[49] 'The Devil, in all his pride, cannot bear the humble heart. If you ask me how it can be known whether a visitation is from me or from the Devil, I answer you that this is the sign. . . . [I]f the soul is in truth visited by me, Eternal Truth, she will at first sight feel holy fear, and with this fear joy and security, together with a sweet prudence that in doubting does not doubt but

and all-fair, is the model and mediatrix of the true theological aesthetic.

St Mark and St John

Mark the Lion and John the Eagle are in conversation about Jesus the Lamb. They are shown in harmony, united in the presence of the Infant Logos, the 'shortened Word' (*verbum abbreviatum*).[50] The almighty Word of the Father, His perfect utterance, is here in summary form, the form of a tiny baby. Explaining why he wants to preach a short sermon on Christmas Day (compassionate Catholic man that he is), St Bernard points to the Word abridged in the manger:

> You ought not to be surprised that I shorten my words, seeing that God the Father has this day shortened His own Word. Do you want to know how long He is, how short the Father made Him? 'I fill Heaven and Earth' (Jer 23:24), says this Word, and now He is made flesh and placed in a narrow manger. 'From eternity', says the Prophet, 'and to eternity thou art God' (Ps 89:2), and behold, He has become a child of one day.[51]

---

through [self-]knowledge deems herself unworthy, saying, "I am not worthy to receive thy visitation, and since I am not worthy, how can such a thing be?" Then she will turn to the vastness of my charity, knowing and seeing that it is possible for me to give, and that I do not look upon her unworthiness, but upon my own worthiness, which makes her worthy of receiving me into herself, by grace and by feeling, since I do not despise the longing with which she calls to me. *And she will humbly receive me, saying, "Behold the handmaid of the Lord, be it done unto me according to thy word"'* (St Catherine of Siena, *Dialogo della divina provvidenza*, chap. 71; ed. G. Cavallini [Rome, 1968], 159).

[50] The reference is to the Vulgate: 'Verbum enim consummans, et abbrevians in aequitate: quia verbum breviatum faciet Dominus super terram': For He shall finish His word and cut it short in justice, because a short word shall the Lord make upon the earth (Rom 9:28; cf. Is 10:22f.).

[51] *In Nativitate Domini sermo 1*, no. 1; *Sancti Bernardi opera*, ed. J. Leclercq and H. Rochais, vol. 4 (Rome, 1966), 243. Cf. Blessed Guerric of Igny, *Sermo 5 in Nativitate Domini*, no. 3; SC 166, 228.

In the Fruit of the Virgin's womb, all the Scriptures come together.[52] In His very person He is the consummation of the Law and the Prophets and the consensus of the Gospels. Mark and John, Matthew and Luke, all four bear harmonious witness to the one Christ and Son and Lord. As St Paschasius said in the ninth century, the Evangelists are gathered in His name, and He is in their midst (cf. Mt 18:20).[53] The Bible is many writings, yet one harmonious whole, the catholicity that is Christ.[54] The Gospel is fourfold but one, and that one Gospel is the Word incarnate. What St Bernard says of the prophecies of the Virgin Birth applies to every inspired text: 'See how beautifully and harmoniously the marvellous deeds and mystical words of the saints sing together.'[55] The words of the Bible broadcast, not a cacophony of contradiction, but a symphony of truth, composed by the Father and conducted by the Holy Spirit in honour of the Son.

Fra Angelico, like the Fathers, finds a beautiful depth and richness in the Scriptures. His painting is proof. With St Augustine, he says of the sacred texts: 'O the profundity, my God, the amazing profundity'.[56] The trees in the background of the altarpiece suggest an image of St Jerome: the Bible is 'an infinite forest of senses' (*infinita sensuum silva*).[57] The Holy Spirit, through the secondary causality of the human authors, has planted a sacred wood of meaning within the Bible, a wood whose rich foliage He opens up in the Tradition of the Church. Like the

[52] As Rupert of Deutz says, 'In the womb of the Virgin, God gathered into one the totality of all Scripture, His whole Word' (*In Isaiam* 2, 31; PL 167, 1362BD).

[53] Cf. *Expositio in Matthaeum* 8, 18; PL 120, 623C.

[54] 'All divine Scripture speaks of Christ, and all divine Scripture is fulfilled in Christ . . . all divine Scripture is that one book which is the Book of Life [viz. Christ]' (Hugh of St Victor, *De arca Noe morali* 2, 9; PL 176, 642D–643A).

[55] *In laudibus Virginis Matris* 2, 11; *Sancti Bernardi opera*, 4:28.

[56] *Confessiones* 12, 14, 17; CCSL 27, 224.

[57] Cited in de Lubac, *Exégèse médiévale*, vol. 1 (Paris, 1959), 119.

Fathers and his Dominican mentors, Fra Angelico reads the Bible for its spiritual as well as its literal sense. Henri de Lubac has shown that the doctrine of the fourfold sense of Scripture, as explained by St Thomas Aquinas, was taught and applied with remarkable fruitfulness in the Florentine communities of the Strict Dominican Observance. Of St Antoninus, de Lubac says:

> The disciple follows the master [Thomas] faithfully, even in the smallest details. What is original about him is that he reproduces the doctrine [of the fourfold sense] in a style more Bonaventuran than Thomist. . . . The hymn he sings to Scripture and its four senses . . . has a freshness of tone that seems to take us back to the past. . . . It is not the announcement of a new spring. But perhaps it is a sign. On the trunk of the faith, even in the least favourable seasons, the branches once more turn green.[58]

Angelico reads the Gospels in the Church, in the light of her faith and liturgy. From her hands he receives the sacred books, and only with her help does he attempt to turn the pages. For him, Catholic belief and worship are the natural environment for exegesis, the only guarantee of a true objectivity. Ruminating daily on the Scriptures in the Divine Office, Fra Angelico trusts the Church to interpret God's Word for Him, for she is the Bride of the Word, one Body with Him, guided by the Holy Spirit into all the truth. The man who would wrench the Scriptures from the hands of the Bride, in the belief that he will thereby become more 'objective' in his reading, traps them and himself beneath the black bushel of subjective opinion. Only from the lampstand of the Church can the light of God's Word scatter the darkness of men's wounded minds.[59]

---

[58] Ibid., 302.

[59] 'The Word is completely unwilling to be kept under a bushel; it wants to be set in a high place, upon the grandeur of the Church's beauty. . . . Let us place it upon the lampstand (I mean, Holy Church), on the heights of true contemplation, where it may kindle for all men the light of the divine dogmas' (St Maximus the Confessor, *Quaestiones ad Thalassium* 63; PG 90, 669A–669D).

St Dominic

Fra Angelico is a Dominican, a son of St Dominic, a friar preacher. He brought men the Word of God in two ways— through the sense of hearing in his sermons and through the sense of sight in his paintings. He 'preached through beauty'.[60] The blessed father Dominic appears in the San Marco altarpiece, as he does in so many of Fra Angelico's other works. He is usually shown at prayer, in one of the postures described in the early Dominican work *The Nine Ways of Prayer of St Dominic*. In the altarpiece he stands in the fifth posture, with hands joined, bearing the lily of virginity. His head is slightly inclined towards St Francis, but he faces the observer, that is to say, the friars who daily prayed before the image. 'The brethren used to be greatly moved to see their father and master . . . , and, for the more devout among them, it was the best possible instruction in how to pray continuously and reverently.'[61]

The two medical martyrs, Cosmas and Damian, appear here as honourary Black Friars. Damian looks up at the Lord Jesus, Cosmas towards us, thereby representing the two elements of the mixed life of St Dominic and his sons: first contemplating and then passing on (through preaching) the fruits of contemplation (*contemplari et contemplata aliis tradere*).

St Thomas Aquinas—The Beauty of the Missing Master

St Thomas Aquinas is Fra Angelico's missing master. According to the art historians, his image was originally on one of the pilasters along the side of the altarpiece.[62] The Angelic Doctor-Friar is without doubt the chief teacher of the Angelic Painter-Friar,

---

[60] See Guy Bédouelle, O.P., *In the Image of Saint Dominic: Nine Portraits of Dominican Life*, (San Francisco, 1994), 71ff.

[61] *The Nine Ways of Prayer of St Dominic* (Dublin, 1978), 32.

[62] Cf. Hood, *Fra Angelico*, 98.

the source of his philosophical and theological aesthetics. As is clear from the *Summa* of St Antoninus, the reformed Dominicans of Florence were enthusiastic Thomists. Brother John never misses an opportunity to paint the figure of Brother Thomas. The most arresting portrait of all is the one in the *Crucifixion* in the San Marco chapterhouse. Kenelm Foster describes it thus:

> The broad face is almost fiercely thoughtful; the eyes express an intense attention and deep longing. It is not hard to imagine that St Thomas really looked like this, in prayer before the crucifix. Let us not think of him as placidly sagacious; nor, even, as some oracular master of all the answers. If he is a prodigious master, it is because he himself is mastered—held by a vision of God's presence in the world's being (*esse*) and fascinated by the mystery of God incarnate and crucified.[63]

The aesthetics of St Thomas is a mustard seed, small and humble, but from it a surprising tree has grown.[64] The Angelic Doctor did not write a separate tract on beauty. The nearest he comes to it is in his commentary on the *Divine Names* of Dionysius the Areopagite. Elsewhere there are only asides and subordinate arguments. And yet, for the last hundred years, these scattered thoughts have proved to be immensely fertile and attractive—not only to philosophers such as Jacques Maritain,[65] but also, among others, to the sculptor Eric Gill, the poet and painter David Jones, and the novelist Flannery O'Connor.[66]

[63] *The Life of St Thomas Aquinas: Biographical Documents* (London and Baltimore, 1959), 22. We are reminded, too, of that 'glowing courtesy' that St Thomas showed to Dante (cf. *Paradiso* 12, 143; *Dantis Aligherii Divina Comoedia edita mandatu Pauli VI Pont. Max.* [Vatican City, 1965], 520).

[64] The definitive study remains F. J. Kovach, *Die Ästhetik des Thomas von Aquin: Eine genetische und systematische Analyse* (Berlin, 1961). See also U. Eco, *The Aesthetics of Thomas Aquinas* (Cambridge, Mass., 1988).

[65] On the aesthetics of Maritain, see A. Rigobello, *Christliche Philosophie im katholischen Denken des 19. und 20. Jahrhunderts*, ed. E. Coreth, W. M. Neidl, and G. Pfligersdorffer (Graz, 1988), 515ff.

[66] See Eric Gill on 'The Beautiful and the Ugly' in *Art* (London, 1934). According to David Jones, the 'formative works' that influenced him were

St Thomas's aesthetics is reserved and modest. There is no
unmanly swooning and mooning. The Dumb Ox is not precious. As a sound Aristotelian, or rather as a good Christian, he
does not despise the beauty humbly known by man's mind
through the senses: 'Pulchra enim dicuntur quae visa placent',
Those things are said to be beautiful that please when seen.[67]
This is the beauty that is connatural to man in his body–soul
unity, the kind he finds it easiest to enjoy. Thomas praises the
beauty of art—of houses and cities, of windows and toys, of
jewels and vases, of paintings and sculpture, of poetic style and
metaphor.[68] He uses analogies drawn from the work of painters
and carpenters.[69] He presents the classical theological defence of
the making and veneration of images.[70] The assured ease with
which he speaks of music proves the soundness of his practical
training at Monte Cassino and his familiarity with the musicol-
ogy of Boethius.[71] In literature, he displays knowledge of the
poets of Rome,[72] and in the Corpus Christi Office, he unfurls
his own marvellous poetic gifts.[73] Thomas is not deaf and blind,

---

'T. E. Hulme and bits of Aristotle and translations of St Thomas, and "the
pseudo-Denis" and Père Maurice de la Taille and von Hügel' (*Dai Greatcoat: A
Self-Portrait of David Jones in His Letters*, ed. R. Hague [London, 1980], 188).
Flannery O'Connor confessed that she cut her 'aesthetic tooth' on Maritain's
Art and Scholasticism. She said she was 'a Thomist three times removed', that is
to say, someone 'who doesn't read Latin or St Thomas but gets it by osmosis'
(*The Habit of Being: Letters*, ed. S. Fitzgerald [New York, 1979], 216, 439).

[67] ST 1a 5, 4, ad 1. Cf. ST 1a2ae 27, 1, ad 3: 'Pulchrum autem dicatur id
cuius ipsa apprehensio placet.'

[68] See the texts listed in Kovach, *Ästhetik*, 93ff.

[69] The artist can do a carving, but not if the wood he uses is knotty and
resists the form he is trying to impose (cf. *3 Sent.*, d. 1, q. 1, a. 1, ad 3).

[70] Cf. ST 2a2ae 94, 2, ad 1; 3a 25, 3.

[71] Cf. *Sententia libri De anima*, lib. 1, lect. 7, no. 9.

[72] For example, with sound judgment, he calls upon Virgil, the prince-poet of
the *lacrimae rerum*, when he is discussing sadness (cf. ST 1a2ae 35, 1, sed contra).

[73] There are solid reasons for supporting the traditional authorship (see J.-P.
Torrell, *Initiation à saint Thomas d'Aquin: Sa personne et son oeuvre* [Fribourg,
1993], 189ff.).

then, to man-made artistic beauty, but the beauty that most interests him is the God-made beauty of being (*esse*) itself, the beauty of all things as they come from the hand of the transcendent Artist, who is in Himself Supersubstantial Beauty, beauty beyond all beauty. Thomas would have agreed with Bonaventure: 'The work of the Supreme Artist is more excellent than any work of human art.'[74]

But what is beauty? In answering that question, Thomas is content to sum up and simplify the definitions that come, through his master Albert, from antiquity, both pagan and Christian. Most frequently, in agreement with Dionysius, he lays down two requirements for beauty:[75] 'radiance' (*claritas*) and 'harmony' (*consonantia*, which he also calls 'due proportion', *debita proportio*).[76] In one important text, he mentions a third hallmark: 'wholeness'(*integritas*).[77] Of these three, the chief is *claritas*, 'radiance'. As Plato and Plotinus saw, as indeed the whole philosophical and poetic tradition of the West has seen, beautiful things *shine*. The loveliness of Fra Angelico's art is lustrous. It illuminates our senses, our imagination, our intellect.

According to St Albert and St Thomas, the radiance of beauty is the splendour of *form*.[78] The form of a thing is its beauty (*decor*).[79] Beauty is *formositas*. The Latin word *forma* means not only

---

[74] *Commentarium in Evangelium Lucae* 12, 39; *Sancti Bonaventurae opera omnia*, vol. 7 (Quaracchi, 1895), 321. This is a comment on Our Lord's words, 'Consider the lilies of the field' (cf. Lk 12:27).

[75] Cf 1 *Sent.*, d. 31, q. 2, a. 1. See Dionysius, *De Divinis Nominibus* 4, 7; PG 3, 701C; cf. St Thomas, *Super librum Dionysii De Divinis Nominibus*, cap. 4, lect. 5. On the various Neoscholastic interpretations of these properties, see Kovach, *Ästhetik*, 18f. For a systematic discussion, see 104ff.

[76] Cf. ST 1a 39, 8.

[77] Ibid.

[78] *Consonantia/proportio* also flows from form, as does *integritas*, which is a kind of proportion (cf. Eco, *Aesthetics*, 83ff., 95ff.). It is form that produces proportion in things.

[79] Cf. 3 *Sent.*, d. 23, q. 3, a. 1, sol. 1, ad 2. 'Beauty properly belongs to the nature of a formal cause' (ST 1a 5, 4, ad 1).

the shape of a material thing but more broadly its outward appearance, how it looks, its good looks, hence its beauty. This is the beauty of what St Thomas calls 'sensible form', the light that is perceptible to the senses.[80] He finds beauty in this outward form, but he wants to plunge more deeply into the intelligible form of a thing, its inward form, the light that enlightens the mind. In a simple, immaterial substance (such as God and the angels), the form is the very nature of the thing, what it is. In composite substances (such as man), the form is what constitutes the nature of the thing, what makes it to be what it is.[81] Thus, in a material substance, as St Albert says, there is beauty when the essence of a thing shines clearly through its outward appearance: beauty is 'the gleaming of the substantial or actual form that is found in the proportioned parts of a material thing'.[82] How it looks clearly reveals what it is. Albert is thinking here of the natural beauty of God-created things, but the definition can be extended, by analogy, to the artificial beauty of man-made things. It is true, as St Thomas says, that all artistic forms are accidental, for only nature can give substantial form.[83] However, art portrays visible subjects in their composite natures, and to this portrayal, by analogy, Albert's definition applies. For example, in Angelico's Madonna, the fairness of her soul, the substantial form, shines through the fineness of her features. Through the material light of his colours (the radiance of Our Lady's Christ-gazing face), through the spatial proportions he has bestowed on her members (the perfect poise of her Christ-bearing arms), we can glimpse the spiritual

[80] Cf. ST 1a 84, 1.

[81] Cf. ibid., 3a 13, 1.

[82] *De pulchro et bono*, q. 1, a. 2. 'The relation of form to matter is not sufficient for the definition [*rationem*] of beauty, unless we bring in the light of form, through which [the form] shines upon the parts of the matter. Then beauty comes forth of itself' (St Albert, *Super librum Dionysium de Divinis Nominibus*, cap. 4, no. 75; *Sancti Doctoris Ecclesiae Alberti Magni opera omnia*, vol. 37/1 [Monasterium Westfalorum, 1972], 185).

[83] Cf. ST 3a 66, 4.

splendour of her pure mind and humble heart. Hopkins says something similar about St Margaret Clitherow, not of her image, but of the woman herself: 'The Christed beauty of her mind/ Her mould of features mated well.'[84]

The philosophical definition of beauty as the splendour of form is also theological. A form is a kind of ray emanating from the brilliant Wisdom of the Creator. 'Every form, by which a thing has being [*esse*], is a participation in the divine brilliance.'[85] In His lovely light we see the light of loveliness. The substantial form of a thing mirrors an eternal idea in the mind of God, an idea contained within *the* Idea, the eternal Word, in whom the Father knows Himself and His creatures.[86] The Word can even be called the uncreated 'form' of all things, 'form' here meaning, not what determines matter, but the exemplar form, the modelling cause of all that is.[87] The form of a thing is its intelligibility, making it to be what it is and so enabling us to see it for what it is. Radiance, the splendour of form, manifests the thing to us. It is its capacity to be known by an intellect. That is why, in St John's Gospel, the incarnate Son reveals the Father by 'glorifying' Him, or, as the Vulgate says, by 'clarifying' Him.[88] To see Him clearly is to know Him as He is.

If beauty is the beauty of form, then beauty is an attribute of being, for form is that 'through which a thing has existence (*esse*)'.[89] Form gives being. Substantial form makes a thing to be

[84] 'Margaret Clitheroe', in Hopkins, *Poetical Works*, 137.

[85] St Albert, *Super librum Dionysii De Divinis Nominibus*, cap. 4, no. 5. Forms are 'nothing other than a kind of seal of the divine knowledge in things' (*De veritate* 2, 1, ad 9).

[86] As a contemporary of Fra Angelico's, Dionysius the Carthusian, says, 'every created thing, insofar as it proportionately imitates the ideal pattern [*rationem idealem*] and exemplar form, which it has in the light and wisdom of the divine mind, is beautiful' (*De venustate mundi et pulchritudine Dei*, a. 1; *Opera omnia*, vol. 34 [Tournai, 1907], 227).

[87] Cf. ST 1a 3, 8, ad 2.

[88] Cf. *De malo* 9, 1; ST 2a2ae 132, 1.

[89] *Super librum Dionysii De Divinis Nominibus*, cap. 4, lect. 5.

the very thing it is, makes a horse a horse, while accidental form makes a thing the way it is, makes a black horse black. Beauty, for Thomas, lies in things themselves, in their being, in their essence and indeed existence. He does not list 'the beautiful' among the so-called 'transcendental' attributes of being, because he is absorbed with the fundamental identity of the good and the beautiful,[90] but there is no doubt that he holds that everything that exists is beautiful, as it is good and true.[91] In fact, for Thomas, as Jacques Maritain says, beauty is 'the splendour of all the transcendentals together',[92] the radiance of the one and the true and the good.

St Thomas regards beauty as a property of being, a feature of reality, whereas the Enlightenment makes it a colourful subjective 'value' pasted over the penny-plain objective 'fact'. For Kant, to say that the San Marco altarpiece is beautiful is merely to voice one's feeling of pleasure at seeing the San Marco altarpiece; nothing in the painting corresponds to the judgement. By contrast, for Thomas, a thing is not beautiful because it is loved; it is loved because it is beautiful.[93] Our minds through our senses perceive the beauty of Angelico's altarpiece; they do not pro-

---

[90] 'The beautiful and the good are identical in the subject, because they are based on the same thing, namely, the form; and that is why the good is praised as beautiful. But they are logically [*ratione*] different, for the good properly relates to the appetite (the good is what all things desire), and therefore it has the character of an end (the appetite being a kind of movement towards a thing). The beautiful, by contrast, relates to the cognitive power, for those things are said to be beautiful that please when seen. Hence the beautiful consists in due proportion, for the senses delight in things duly proportioned, as in things like unto themselves (the senses, too, are a sort of reason, as is every knowing power). Now, since knowing takes place through assimilation, and since similitude relates to form, beauty properly belongs to the nature of a formal cause' (ST 1a 5, 4, ad 1).

[91] On the controversy about the 'transcendentality' of beauty, see Kovach, *Ästhetik*, 183ff., and Eco, *Aesthetics*, 20ff.

[92] *Art and Scholasticism*, 172. Balthasar says that, for Thomas, the *pulchrum* is 'within and yet beyond the transcendentals' (H 3/1/1, 360; GL 4, 400).

[93] *Super librum Dionysii De Divinis Nominibus*, cap. 4, lect. 10.

duce it. Beauty is not read into works of art, God's and men's; it radiates out of them. As Gerard Manley Hopkins says, it 'keeps warm/ Men's wits to the things that are'.[94]

According to Balthasar, the metaphysics of St Thomas is 'the philosophical reflection of the free glory of the living God of the Bible and thus the interior completion of ancient (and thus human) philosophy'.[95] The doctrine of the real distinction between *esse* and *essentia* makes possible a superbly clear differentiation between the beauty ('glory') of God and the beauty of the world.[96] However, Balthasar also claims that St Thomas's philosophical aesthetic 'failed to achieve a theological translation, that is, to be seen as the unfolding of a theology based on the Biblical revelation'.[97] I hope to show that this second judgment is not correct. I shall be arguing that Fra Angelico's art has its source in a Thomistic aesthetic that is theological as well as philosophical. Moreover, like Balthasar's, it has at its centre the Johannine paradox of glory and humiliation: the beauty of the Three-Personed God shining from the crucified form of the incarnate Son.

St Francis

Francis and Dominic, founders of orders that sometimes clashed in scholarly disputation, were united in their religious resolution to abandon everything and, in poverty, to follow the poor Christ. The spiritual bond between the founders of the two mendicant orders (who, by tradition, once met at Perugia) is often displayed in Fra Angelico's work. Something similar takes place in Dante's *Paradiso*, where Thomas sings the praises of Francis and Bonaventure of Dominic. To the reformed Domini-

---

[94] 'To What Serves Mortal Beauty?', in Hopkins, *Poetical Works*, 182f.
[95] H 3/1/1, 366; GL 4, 405f.
[96] Cf. H 3/1/1, 356; GL 4, 395.
[97] H 2, 19; GL 2, 21.

cans, Francis, too, was a beloved father, the exemplary spouse of
that Lady Poverty whose hand they had taken. As Dante makes
Thomas say of Francis:

> And unto her he pledged his wedded faith
> In spiritual court and *coram patre* too,
> And loved her more each day that he drew breath.[98]

For Angelico, as for Dominic and Francis, poverty is not an
ideological obsession but a Christological devotion. In the likeness of the divine Bridegroom, with Him and for love of Him,
they espouse the beautiful poverty of the manger and the Cross.

3. The Beauty of Christ

Fra Angelico's art is centred on Christ. 'His painting', says Father
Guy Bédouelle, 'never ceases to speak of the Incarnation.'[99] He
displays, before our dazzled eyes, the rich mysteries of the incarnate Word. In many of them, Dominican saints join the original
actors of the drama. Dominic kneels on Calvary or stands on
Tabor. Peter Martyr waits in the wings of Bethlehem. Fra
Angelico is teaching us a theological lesson: in their historical
circumstances, the mysteries of the life of Jesus are past, but,
through the glorification of His crucified body, by the working
of the Holy Spirit, they live for ever in the Church's liturgy as
sources of truth and causes of grace.[100]

The San Marco altarpiece represents the Word made flesh in
His infancy. This little boy is God. The halo behind His head
bears the mark of the Cross, the sign in the Middle Ages of a
Divine Person, One of the Trinity. He is God the Son, who,
without ceasing to be true God, has been made true man for us in

---

[98] *Paradiso* 11, 61ff.; *The Comedy of Dante Alighieri, the Florentine*, trans. Dorothy L. Sayers and Barbara Reynolds (Baltimore, 1962), 150.

[99] Bédouelle, *Image*, 77.

[100] Cf. CCC 512ff.

the Virgin's womb. This Child is Priest: His right hand is raised in blessing. And He is King: He holds the orb, the whole world, in His hands. Angels, like courtiers, bear the instruments of His Passion. A small crucifix is superimposed upon the larger scene. In the original layout of the altar, there was also a magnificent Entombment, in which the dead cruciform body of the Son of God is held up by Joseph of Arimathea and worshipped by Mary and John. Fra Angelico is once again preaching a sermon: In the flesh that He took from the Virgin, the Son of God truly suffered and died; in that flesh He rose from the tomb and ascended to the Father; and with that flesh He feeds us at the altar.

Beauty is a theme, as well as a quality, of the painting. The Child-God is a Burning Babe, a central fire, inflaming the saints with His brightness. Fra Angelico shows Him as Dominicans sing of Him in the Office of Christmas Day: 'Thou art beautiful above the sons of men; grace is poured abroad in thy lips' (Ps 44:3). Behind his throne, we catch sight of cypresses and orange trees, a clear sky and a still ocean. The material world is already beautiful through its creation, says Angelico, but, through the Incarnation of the Son of God, through His Cross and Resurrection from the tomb, it is raised up to a loveliness beyond compare.

The Beauty of the Triune God

The altarpiece gently suggests the beauty of the Triune God. To a Dominican mind familiar with St Catherine of Siena, the 'pacific sea' in the background would be a symbol of God the Father.[101] In any case, in every icon, the Virgin and Child bear witness to the Trinity, as Pope John Paul II explains in one of his catecheses:

[101] 'Rise up, then, promptly and follow Him, for no one can come to me, the Father, except by Him. He is the Way and the Door by which you must enter into me, the Pacific Sea [*mare pacifico*]' (*Dialogo*, chap. 100, 239).

The traditional iconography, which shows Mary with the child Jesus in her arms and does not picture Joseph beside her, constitutes a silent but firm statement of her virginal motherhood and, for that very reason, of the Son's divinity. This image, therefore, could be called the icon of Christ's divinity.[102]

The human Mother in a way testifies to the divine Father. As the Fathers of the Church say, the one person of God the Son is begotten eternally of the Father without a mother in His divinity and born in time of the Mother without a father in His humanity. Later images of St Joseph do not clash with this testimony, because he usually carries the lily of purity. He is Our Lady's spouse most chaste.

All the Church's Fathers and Doctors present a 'theological aesthetic'; in some the note of beauty is more accented, in none is it wholly absent. The theologian-saints of the Tradition are men transported by the transcendent beauty of God, the glory of the Trinity shining in the human face of the Son. They are astonished and overwhelmed by the splendour of divinely revealed truth. The conversion of an Augustine is not from aesthetics to religion but from a lower to a higher aesthetics, to the 'Beauty so ancient and so new' revealed in the humble Jesus.[103] The mystic who humbles himself behind the name 'Dionysius the Areopagite', and whom Fra Angelico, through Albert and Thomas, would have known well (the San Marco library had no fewer than seven copies of his works),[104] gives us the first principle of every theological aesthetic: God is 'supersubstantial beauty' (*to hyperousion kalon*), 'superbeauty' (*hyperkalon*), the source of all beautiful things.[105]

---

[102] General Audience Address (May 23, 1990), no. 3; *Insegnamenti di Giovanni Paolo II* 12/1 (1990), 1378f.

[103] *Confessiones* 10, 27, 38; CCSL 27, 175. Cf. H 2, 97; GL 2, 95.

[104] B. Ullman and P. A. Stadter, *The Public Library of Renaissance Florence* (Padua, 1972), 134f.

[105] *De Divinis Nominibus*, cap. 4, no. 7; PG 3, 701CD.

Beauty is an essential attribute of God and therefore common to the Three Divine Persons.[106] However, the Christian Tradition—from Augustine and Hilary to Peter Lombard, Albert, Thomas, and Bonaventure—holds that it can be appropriated in a special way to the Second Person. In his treatise on the Trinity in the First Part of the *Summa Theologiae*, St Thomas says that all three of the hallmarks of beauty are to be found in God the Son. First, radiance (*claritas*) is found in Him, because He is the Word of the Father. When we speak intelligently and thus intelligibly, the light of the mind shines through our words and gives them clarity. If our thinking is clear, so are our words. Similarly, the Word eternally uttered by the Father completely and perfectly expresses Him; He reflects, He is, the brightness of the Father's mind. Secondly, due proportion (*debita proportio*) is to be found in God the Son, because He is the perfect image of the Father. In fact, says St Thomas, if an image is a perfect likeness of the original, we call it beautiful even if the thing it copies is ugly. As the perfect consubstantial image of the Father, the Son is divine beauty. Thirdly, the Son has wholeness (*integritas*) because He has in Himself the whole nature of the Father. In eternally begetting the Son, the Father communicates the whole of the divine essence; nothing is missing in what is received by the Son, nor is anything lost in its giving by the Father.[107]

---

[106] St Thomas points out that Job is told to 'clothe' himself with beauty, but that God Himself is not 'clothed' with beauty. No, 'His very essence is beauty' (cf. *In Iob* 40). Indeed, 'God is the very essence of beauty' (*Compendium theologiae* 2, 9). In other words, God is beautiful by essence; His creatures are beautiful by participation in His beauty.

[107] Cf. ST 1a 39, 8. On the Son as the Image and therefore the Beauty of the Father, see also St Bonaventure, *1 Sent.*, d. 31, p. 2, a. 1, q. 3, in *Sancti Bonaventurae opera omnia*, vol. 1 (Quaracchi, 1882), 544.

The Beauty of Creation

Pagan antiquity never attained a coherent doctrine of creation. The mind of Plotinus soared up towards Absolute Beauty, but he could not see the beauty of the world as the free and loving *gift* of that Beauty. His theological aesthetic is, therefore, deficient in *gratitude*. 'Through the things He had made' says St Augustine, '[the Greek philosophers] arrived at a knowledge of the God who made things, but "they did not honour Him as God *or give thanks*" (cf. Rom 1:21ff.).'[108]

With the insight of grateful love, St Thomas and St Bonaventure, following St Augustine, teach that all things bear a trace (*vestigium*) of the Trinitarian Beauty that created them. However, among visible creatures, man alone is made in the image of God's beauty.[109] For the majority of the Fathers, the image of God, and therefore the mirror of the Trinity's beauty, is to be found chiefly in man's rational spiritual soul,[110] by which he is *capax Dei*, capable of knowing and loving the God of Wisdom and Love who made him. St Thomas is of the same opinion: 'We find in man a likeness to God by way of an image in his mind, but in the other parts of his being by way of trace.'[111] However, he does not exclude the body altogether from the dignity of the image: 'The soul united with the body is more like God than the soul separated from the body, because it possesses its nature in a more complete fashion.'[112] And he agrees with St Augustine that man's upright bodily stature is an outward sign of his mind's capacity for contemplation.[113] 'The very shape of the human body repre-

---

[108] *Sermo 241*, 3; PL 38, 1135.

[109] Cf. ST 1a 93, 6; 45, 7.

[110] St Augustine asks: 'Where is the image of God in man?' 'In the mind', he replies, 'in the intellect' (*In Iohannis Evangelium tractatus 3*, 4; CCSL 36, 22).

[111] ST 1a 93, 6.

[112] *De potentia* 5, 10, ad 5.

[113] Cf. *De diversis quaestionibus lxxxiii*, 51, 3; CCSL 44A, 80f.

sents, by way of trace, the image of God in the soul.'[114] The body as trace is an image of the image. This is man's singular glory: to be like God by both image and trace.

The parallelism 'image and likeness' suggested to many of the Fathers a double original beauty in Adam. The 'image' is the splendour of his nature, especially his soul, whose threefold faculties, according to St Augustine, mirror its Three-Personed Maker. The 'likeness' is the supernatural gift of divinizing grace, a partaking of the life of the Triune God. St Thomas, following Peter Lombard, distinguished between the 'image of creation' in man's nature and the 'image of recreation' in grace. Adam was created in grace, says St Thomas,[115] and therefore in supernatural beauty. By the gratuitous gifts that make up the state of Original Justice, our first parents lived in harmony with God, with each other, and within themselves. Adam's reason was subject to God, his lower powers to reason, and his body to his soul. He dwelt in a lovely place, in an earthly, bodily Paradise, which lay to the East, that most excellent part of the earth (says Thomas, quoting Aristotle), 'the right hand of Heaven'.[116]

When he sinned, Adam lost the gifts of original beauty—grace, freedom from concupiscence, and bodily immortality—for himself and for us, plunging us into the ugliness of sin and death. According to St Thomas, formally speaking, Original Sin is the lack or privation of Original Justice,[117] a 'disordered disposition arising from the dissolving of that harmony [*harmoniae*] in which the essence of Original Justice consisted.'[118] Adam's descendants come into existence bereft of the first fairness, deprived of the beautifying grace of the Holy Spirit. The disfig-/ urement is not an intrinsic corruption but rather the disarray

[114] ST 1a 93, 6, ad 3.
[115] Ibid., 95, 1.
[116] Ibid., 102. 1, citing *De caelo* 2, 2; 285b16.
[117] ST 1a2ae 82, 3.
[118] Ibid., 82, 1

that comes from the loss of a gift. Using a phrase that he ascribes to St Bede, St Thomas compares fallen Adam to the man who fell among thieves: he is stripped of gratuitous gifts, wounded in his nature.[119]

The Trinitarian God of glory did not abandon Adam's race to sin and death and the befouling captivity of Satan. In the fulness of time, the Father sent His eternal Son, His radiant Image, to take flesh from the all-fair Virgin of Nazareth. He came to liberate man from the dis-grace of unlikeness and to lead him to the clear Kingdom of the Father.[120] The work of redemption is one of rebeautification. As St Thomas says, the Incarnation 'refashions all human nature'.[121] Just as the idea (or 'word') in the artist's mind is the model for his work of art, so the divine Word, the Father's Eternal Idea, is the model for all creation. Now when the artist's work of art is damaged, he repairs it on the model of his original idea. Similarly, through the uniting of human nature to the eternal Word, the Father restores the damaged masterpiece of fallen mankind.[122]

The Beauty of the Incarnate Word

Christ is beautiful in His divine nature, but He is also beautiful in His lowly human nature, 'fairer than all the sons of men' (cf. Ps 44:3). In his commentary on Psalm 44, St Thomas quotes St Augustine:

[119] Ibid., 85, 1.

[120] As St Athanasius says in his *De Incarnatione*: 'As when a figure which has been painted on wood is spoilt by dirt, it is necessary for him whose portrait it is to come again so that the picture can be renewed in the same material . . . even so the all-holy Son of the Father, who is the image of the Father, came to our realms to renew man who had been made in His likeness, and, as one lost, to find Him through the forgiveness of sins' (no. 14; ed. R. W. Thomson [Oxford, 1971], 167).

[121] ST 3a 2, 11.

[122] Ibid., 3a 3, 8.

He is beautiful in the womb of the Virgin, where, without losing His divinity, He assumed humanity. He is beautiful when
born, the infant Word . . . beautiful in His parents' arms, beautiful in His miracles, . . . beautiful in laying down His life, beautiful in taking it up again.[123]

'He is beautiful when born, the infant Word', the *Verbum
infans*, the wordless Word. That is how we see Him in the San
Marco altarpiece. The Art of the Father is now an artless Babe.
Eve sought beauty in forbidden fruit, says St Thomas, 'yet fairer
still is the Virgin's Fruit on whom the angels long to gaze.'[124] St
Cosmas is pointing to Him, as if to say: 'Unless you be converted and become like this little Child, you shall not enter
into the Kingdom of Heaven' (Mt 18:3). In his commentary
on St Matthew's Gospel,[125] St Thomas mentions the various
Patristic opinions about the identity of the child blessed by
Our Lord and made a symbol of discipleship. Some believe
that it was an actual child, St Martial, who later became a disciple of St Peter and preached the gospel in Gaul. But others
maintain that the child is the Son of God Himself, He who,
without losing His grandeur as God, made Himself little as
man in the womb of the Virgin. This is the opinion of St Bernard in a Christmas Eve sermon. The speechless Logos by His
infancy teaches us to be humble. The rivers of grace cannot
flow uphill, says St Bernard, up the steep cliff of the proud
man's heart. Only when we are little and lowly can the gravity
of grace fall upon us. 'I am among you as one who serves' (Lk
20:27).[126]

---

[123] *Enarrationes in Psalmos* 44, 3; CCSL 38, 496. See Carol Harrison, *Beauty
and Revelation in the Thought of St Augustine* (Oxford, 1992), passim.

[124] *In Salutationem Angelicam*, no. 3. The Blessed Virgin was filled with light,
says Thomas, when, by the Holy Spirit, she conceived Christ, who is 'the
Splendou. of the Father's glory' (*3 Sent.*, d. 3, q. 1, a. 2, sed contra 2).

[125] Cf. *Super Evangelium Matthaei*, cap. 18, lect. 1.

[126] *In Vigilia Nativitatis sermo 4*; *Sancti Bernardi opera*, 4: 226f.

According to St Thomas, there is a fourfold beauty in Christ.[127] First, in His divine nature (*secundum divinam formam*) He has beauty, for He is God the Son, the Splendour of the Father. Secondly, in His human nature He has the beauty of grace and the virtues, for He is 'full of grace and truth'. Thirdly, in Christ we see the beauty of moral conduct (*conversationis honestae*); the human actions of the Son of God are more upright and therefore more beautiful than any other man's. Finally, Christ as man, even before His Resurrection, had beauty of body, a beauty befitting the man who was God, in whose face the spiritual beauty of the Godhead shone. He is the Bridegroom who delights the Bride: 'Behold, thou art fair, my Beloved' (Song 1:15). His voice was lovely because what He said was both pleasing and useful. He had an orderly and fervent manner of speech, teaching with authority. And yet Christ's visible beauty was not the kind the world acclaims. He did not have 'golden hair and a ruddy complexion'. He was poor and did not wear fine clothes. Israel's true Messiah was no dandy. However, says Thomas, quoting Augustine, 'something divine shone from His face.'[128] The face, that marvellous fragment of flesh that in every man is the expression of the person, in Christ manifested Him as who He is, the Father's eternal Son.

Christ is beautiful, and He comes to restore us to beauty. The eternal Word through whom man was formed is made flesh to re-form him,[129] to rescue him from the repulsiveness of sin and death. But He beautifies the world in a marvellous way, through a 'wonderful exchange'.[130] The radiant Son of the Father be-

---

[127] *In Psalmos* 44, 2.

[128] Ibid.

[129] 'Ipse ad eam venit reformator, qui erat eius ante formator' (*Enarrationes in Psalmos* 32, 2, 2, 16; CCSL 38, 266).

[130] On the theme of the *admirabile commercium* in Patristic Christology, see Hans Urs von Balthasar, *Die Handlung*, vol. 3 of *Theodramatik* (Einsiedeln, 1980), 226ff.; ET: *Theo-Drama: Theological Dramatic Theory*, vol. 4: *The Action* (San Francisco, 1994), 246ff.

comes the Suffering Servant, without form or comeliness (cf. Is 53:2); the spotless Lamb takes on the hideous sin of the world, so that the unlovely sons of Adam may be re-formed as the glorious children of God.[131] This is the central paradox of the 'theological aesthetic' of St John's Gospel, of the Fathers, and of the whole Tradition: the revelation of Trinitarian glory, the divine form, in the humbled human form of God the Son.

St Thomas keeps in mind the great paradox of St John's Gospel—the coincidence, in the incarnate Word, of glory and humiliation. Through its union with His Divine Person, the human soul of the Son of God enjoyed from conception the glorifying vision of the Father.[132] Even before the Resurrection, Christ in His human soul was *simul comprehensor et viator*, at once beholding the Father and travelling to that goal.[133] However, by a divine ordinance, to which He assented with His human will, glory did not overflow from the summit of His soul onto its lower slopes—except on one occasion, at the Transfiguration, which was a foreshadowing of the radiance of the Resurrection.[134] The Son of God took the lowly way, the way of the Cross. He assumed the condition of a slave. He did not dazzle men with His greatness.

It is the unfailing remembrance of Our Lord's self-emptying that explains the restraint of St Thomas's theological aesthetic. How, he asks, could Christ be beautiful in His Passion? After all, does not Isaiah say: 'There is no beauty in Him, nor comeliness' (Is 53:2)? Actually, there was beauty in Him, says St Thomas in his commentary on Isaiah, 'but it was hidden because of the infirmity He assumed; He had loveliness, . . . but it was ob-

---

[131] As St Augustine says, 'He in whom we believe gave them power to become the sons of God. The beautiful Bridegroom appeared ugly on account of our ugliness, because "we saw Him", and "He had neither form nor comeliness"' (*Enarrationes in Psalmos* 83, 11; CCSL 39, 1158).

[132] Cf. ST 3a 34, 4.

[133] Ibid., 15, 10.

[134] Ibid., 45, 2.

scured because of the poverty He preserved.' Unlike Priam, whose outward magnificence gleamed upon all, the King of Kings chose to humble and empty Himself.[135] His human nature does not have all the perfections it could have, all the visible beauty to which it is entitled. The Trinity freely wills that the Son should assume our human nature with certain disabilities (*defectus*), because He comes to save us by a most marvellous exchange: the bearing and bearing away of sin, the taking of death and the giving of life.[136]

The body of Jesus was disfigured in dying but of supreme beauty in rising again. The lower the black depths to which, in the flesh, He went down, the higher the bright peaks to which, in the flesh, He rose. The glorious body of the Son of God is beautiful. Its principal attribute is *claritas*, radiance, the prerequisite of beauty.[137] Our Lord's resurrected flesh was steeped in this coruscating light even during the Forty Days before the Ascension, but, according to the Fathers, it was hidden from the eyes of the disciples.[138] St Cyril of Alexandria suggests that the brightness of the risen body—Christ's and ours—was revealed in advance at the Transfiguration in order to strengthen the Apostles' faith. Even on Tabor, they fell on their faces. They could not bear the weight of glory. After the Resurrection, Our Lord's chief task was to assure them of the reality of the risen body, and so He showed Himself in a humble and homely way, without the outward blaze of beauty.[139]

[135] *Postilla super Isaiam*, cap. 53. St Albert says that, in the eyes of unbelievers, Our Lord was 'befouled by the vile spitting of the Jews . . . and died pallid on the Cross', but to believers, He was 'beautiful in every state' (*Commentarii in primam partem Psalmorum* 44, 3; *Beati Alberti Magni opera omnia*, ed. A. Borgnet, vol. 15 [Paris, 1892], 666).

[136] Cf. ST 3a qq. 14 and 15.

[137] Ibid., 54, 2, ad 1.

[138] 'The weakness of their human sight could not have borne to look upon it. At that moment the important thing was that His disciples should direct their gaze on Him, so that they might recognize Him' (ibid.).

[139] *In Joannis Evangelium*, lib. 12 (20:19, 20); PG 74, 705BC.

Noli me tangere.

The risen body of Jesus also has integrity; it is whole and complete. St Thomas says that it keeps the marks of the Passion not only for proof that it is the very same body that was nailed and lanced but also as a mark of 'special beauty', as a dashing emblem of the God-Man's trampling upon death.[140] This Thomistic insight finds its way into Angelico's art. In the *Noli me tangere* fresco in San Marco, the smudges of red paint used for the spring flowers of the Easter garden are repeated in the wounds of the risen Gardener, as if to say: 'His flesh has flowered again like the rose.'[141]

4. The Beauty of Christ's Saints

The Beauty of the Saints by Grace

Light streams from the Burning Babe. He seems to be all gold, shedding His gleams on all the saints, those who, as Dante says, 'with His Blood He made His Bride.'[142] They are beautiful with His beauty. 'And the city hath no need of the sun, nor of the moon, to shine it. For the glory of God hath enlightened it; and the Lamb is the lamp thereof' (Rev 21:23). St Bonaventure provides a commentary on the scene:

> That city is beautified and lit up by the light of the Lamb, for His divinity is there in place of the sun, His humanity in place of the moon, and the blessed in place of the stars. And so, by reason of this beauty, there is no need of sun or moon. The Sun or Lamb Himself is the source of the beauty. He is the 'bright-

[140] Cf. ST 3a 54, 4, ad 1. The sacred scars of the Son are a constant supplication before the Father, as St Catherine says, 'continually crying for mercy' (*Dialogo*, chap. 41; p. 88).

[141] An image St Bonaventure uses (cf. *Feria 2 post Pascha sermo*, in *Opera omnia*, vol. 9 [Quaracchi, 1901], 283A). See Didi-Huberman, *Fra Angelico*, 13–27.

[142] *Paradiso* 31, 1; 660.

ness' and the substance 'of eternal light and the mirror without spot' (Wis 7:26).[143]

The Bridegroom-Lamb is all fair, and He wants His Bride, the Church and her members, to reflect His fairness. In his treatise on grace, St Thomas says that there is diversity in the grace that God pours out on men because He wants 'the beauty and perfection of the Church to merge from the array of these different degrees'.[144] St Albert compares the diversity in glory of the heavenly Church to the varied blooms of a garden:

> In the Kingdom of Christ there are many different flowers. There we find Jesus, the most beautiful flower of all. He is 'beautiful above the sons of men' (Ps 44:3). That is why He calls Himself a flower in the Canticle: 'I am the flower of the fields', He says, 'and the lily of the valleys' (2:1). There, too [in Heaven], the undefiled Virgin Mary is a flower of the greatest beauty and sweetness. There the Martyrs are red like the roses. There the Confessors are verdant like the violet. There the Virgins glow white like the lily.[145]

Everything in Christ is for sharing: both the beauty of His grace and the radiance of His Resurrection. The incarnate Word is 'full of grace and truth' (cf. Jn 1:14), and that grace overflows to us, grace upon grace (Jn 1:16). St Thomas expresses this truth by saying that the personal grace of Christ, the Sanctifying Grace with which the human soul of the Son of God is filled beyond measure, is really identical with His grace as Head of the Church.[146] The living waters of the Holy Spirit flow from the human Heart of the Father's Son. Sanctifying Grace is truly the grace of *Christ*. It is merited by Him, and it makes us like Him, so

---

[143] *In Festo Omnium Sanctorum sermo 2*, in *Opera omnia*, 9:601.
[144] ST 1a2ae 112, 4. The translation is that of my teacher and friend the late Fr Cornelius Ernst, O.P. (St Thomas Aquinas, *The Gospel of Grace*, vol. 30 of *Summa Theologiae* [London, 1972], 155).
[145] *Sermo 49 De Beata Caecilia; Beati Alberti Magni opera omnia*, 13:605.
[146] Cf. ST 3a 8, 5.

that what He is by nature, we become by grace. Adoptive sonship, says St Thomas, 'is a certain likeness of the natural Sonship'.[147] By the grace of our Baptism, we are sons-in-the-Son.

Now the Son is beauty, and so it follows that the sons-in-the-Son will share His beauty. To quote St Thomas again, 'man is made like to the splendour of the eternal Son through the brightness of grace, which is attributed to the Holy Spirit.'[148] The Angelic Doctor shows his debt to the Greek Fathers when he expounds the beautifying and divinizing effects of *gratia gratum faciens*, the grace that makes us pleasing to God, the Sanctifying Grace of the Holy Spirit.[149] St Thomas has a 'theological aesthetic' of grace. He does not forget that *gratia*, like *charis*, means loveliness and charm as well as gift and favour. When explaining what is meant by saying that grace is a quality, St Thomas cites the Gloss (the medieval line-by-line commentary on Scripture): 'Grace is the radiance of the soul, attracting holy love.' He then goes on to say: 'But radiance of soul is a quality, just like beauty of body.'[150] Sanctifying Grace is divinizing grace, a participation in the divine nature (cf. 2 Pet 1:4), a share in the life of the Triune God. Now the divine nature is beautiful; the Triune God is superbeauty; and so the divinized soul is divinely beautiful. 'Beauty of soul consists in being made like God.'[151]

[147] Ibid., 24, 3. Cf. 3a 3, 5, ad 2.

[148] Ibid., 23, 2, ad 3.

[149] For example, St Cyril of Alexandria says: 'We who bear the image of the Earthly Man cannot escape corruption unless the beauty of the image of the Heavenly Man is imprinted upon us, through our call to adoption as God's sons. Partaking of [Christ] through the Spirit, we are sealed in Him, in His likeness and to the archetype of the image. . . . Thus *the ancient beauty of nature is restored*' (*In Joannis Evangelium*, lib. 1 [1, 12]; PG 73, 153B). And again, St Cyril asks: 'What confers on us the divine image and imprints, like a seal, the *superterrestrial beauty*, if not the Spirit?' (*De SS. Trinitate dialogus* 7; PG 75, 1088B).

[150] ST 1a2ae 110, 2. 'Grace is called by the saints the "health and loveliness of the soul" ' (*4 Sent.*, d. 1, q. 1, a. 2, obj. 1).

[151] *4 Sent.*, d. 18, q. 1, a. 2, sol. 1. Writing to Sister Agnes of Jesus-Mary, Blessed Elizabeth of the Trinity says: 'Through all things, by day and by night,

The saints owe everything to Christ. They are the men and women in whom His divinizing, beautifying grace is most resplendent. They are the Father's great work of art, human beings who have let the Holy Spirit purge and fashion them into the likeness of the incarnate Son, changed from glory to glory. Their souls, to quote Hopkins' phrase again, have a 'Christed beauty'.[152]

The Beauty of the Virtues of the Saints

The virtues shine dazzlingly, heroically, in the lives of the saints. St Thomas says that virtuous conduct is beautiful because reason gives it radiance and good proportions.[153] Vice, by contrast, is disorder and deformity: the sinner is 'deprived of the comeliness of grace by the ugliness of sin'.[154] Fra Angelico shows this in his painting—in the disembodied spitting head and hitting hands in *The Mocking of Christ*,[155] or in the soldier-scorpions, in *The Carrying of the Cross*, pushing away the Blessed Virgin.[156]

According to St Thomas, the morally right and honourable, the *honestum*, is identical with the beautiful (the *decorum*).[157] There is beauty in all the virtues but especially in temperance. Temperance implies moderation and therefore harmony, due proportion—the hallmark of beauty. The temperate man controls the passions that, once out of hand, make us ugly and brutish. The

in clear light or in darkness, let us live like the Magdalen, always under the eyes of Unchangeable Beauty, who wants to fascinate us, to captivate us, more than that, *to deify us*' (Letter 121, *Oeuvres complètes* [Paris, 1991], 406). I am grateful to Mother Pia, O.C.D., of the Philadelphia Carmel for pointing out this text to me.

[152] 'Margaret Clitheroe', in Hopkins, *Poetical Works*, 137.

[153] Cf. ST 2a2ae 145, 2.

[154] Ibid., 1a2ae 109, 7.

[155] Cell 7 in San Marco.

[156] In the so-called *Armadio degli argenti* at San Marco.

[157] Cf. ST 2a2ae 145, 2.

light of reason shines through the ordering of his passions.[158] Virginity, as a kind of chastity, has a most excellent beauty. St Thomas quotes St Ambrose: 'Who can find a greater beauty than the comeliness of the virgin, who is loved by the King, approved by the Judge, dedicated to the Lord, consecrated to God?'[159]

There is beauty in the natural moral virtues, those a man acquires by his own unaided efforts, but there is even greater beauty in the infused moral virtues, the virtues of a man who is divinized by the grace of Christ, virtues animated by the Holy Spirit's poured-in gift of charity. Charity, says St Thomas, is the 'form' of the virtues.[160] It shapes them, elevates them, sweeps them up into new heights of spiritual beauty. The moral virtues direct a man to their own proper object; charity takes them up to the end of ends, to the superbeauty of the Trinity. The saints are lovely because they love.[161]

The Beauty of the Saints in Glory

Grace, said St Thomas, is the beginning of glory in us.[162] The beautifying work of the risen Lord starts in this life in the sanctification of men and reaches its fulfilment in the life to come in their glorification—in the Beatific Vision, the Communion of Saints, the resurrection of the body, and the life everlasting. Christ, who now beautifies the souls of His saints, will on the

[158] Ibid., 145, 4.

[159] Ibid., 2a2ae 152, 5 (see St Ambrose, *De virginibus* 1, 7; PL 16, 210B).

[160] Ibid., 1a2ae 23, 8. Cf. *3 Sent.*, d. 23, q. 3, a. 1, sol. 1, ad 2.

[161] 'The soul is the image of Incarnate Truth by means of the virtues that it has, not from itself, but infused by God. This makes the rational soul still lovelier, because grace, from which come the virtues, is more powerful than nature. And thus the soul is the image of Incarnate Truth, that is Christ, as St Paul says, "Those whom He foreknew, He predestined to be conformed to the image of His Son"' (St Antoninus, *Summae sacrae theologiae iuris pontificii et caesarei pars quarta* [Venice, 1571], 2).

[162] Cf. ST 2a2ae 24, 3.

last day beautify their bodies. The Word made flesh is the Head, and we are His members; His victory over death is, therefore, ours too.[163] Why was it necessary for Christ to rise again? Among other reasons, answers St Thomas, 'because of us, so that a glorious Resurrection might begin in the Head which was later to be in the members.'[164] It is 'our lowly nature', says Pope St Leo the Great, which in Christ is raised far above all the angels at the Father's right hand.[165] The glory that now belongs to the flesh of Christ is destined to be given to all the just on the last day, when He 'changes our lowly body to be like His glorious body' (cf. Phil 3:21). The whole man is destined to share in the beauty of the Trinity.

According to St Thomas, following the Apostle Paul and all the Fathers, the Resurrection of Christ is the efficient and exemplary cause of our resurrection.[166] His flesh is endowed with indestructible loveliness, and so too will ours be when He comes again. Now beauty is integrity; where wholeness is impaired, beauty is destroyed. It follows, therefore, according to St Thomas, that, in the resurrection, Christ will make our bodies lovely like His own and therefore entire and complete. By the power of God, everything belonging by nature to the body will be restored. The whole man rises, and therefore all the parts of his body.[167] Some parts of the body will no longer be functionally

---

[163] As St Augustine explains to his catechumens: 'We also believe in the resurrection of the body that has first come out of Christ, so that the Body also may hope for what has already been done for the Head. The Head of the Church is Christ: the Church is the Body of Christ. Our Head is risen and has ascended into Heaven. Where the Head is, there also the members will be' (*De symbolo ad catechumenos* 1, 9; CCSL 46, 199).

[164] *3 Sent.*, d. 21, q. 2, a. 1. Cf. ST 3a 53, 1.

[165] *Tractatus 74*; CCSL 138A, 455.

[166] Cf. ST 3a 56, 1.

[167] 'Whatever belongs to the nature of the human body was whole in the body of the risen Christ. Now it is obvious that flesh and bones and blood and other such things belong to the nature of the human body. Therefore, all these things were in the body of the risen Christ. And they were there whole and

necessary, but they will not for that reason be removed; they will be there, says St Augustine, 'for their loveliness, not their useful-ness; for the display of beauty, not the service of need'.[168] Every-thing unsightly will be remedied. Lack of limb or organ will be supplied; ugly excess will be diminished. There will be 'no cor-ruption, no ugliness, no defect'.[169] Whether they died young or old, even if they were killed in the womb, all men will be raised up with bodies in the perpetual vigour of youth, *in aetate Christi*, at that age at which Christ rose from the grave.[170] According to the Schoolmen, following St Augustine, the distinguishing fea-tures of masculinity and femininity will be preserved; men will be raised as men, women as women. Women will be adorned with a new beauty, which will no longer arouse desire but only praise for the wisdom and goodness of God who made what was not and purifies what He made.[171] There will be nothing unbe-coming. The body, perfectly submissive to the glorified soul, will be everlastingly lovely. All tears will be wiped away, every sick-ness healed.[172] The bodies of the martyrs will keep the scars of their sufferings, just as the risen flesh of Jesus bears for ever the mark of nails and lance; but, for them as for Him, this will be a jewel of 'special loveliness', an adornment, not a deformity.[173] The gash on Peter Martyr's head is a scarlet crown.

---

complete, without any diminishing. The Resurrection would not have been perfect if what in death had fallen had not been restored' (ST 3a 54, 3; cf. *4 Sent.*, d. 44, q. 1, a. 2, sol. 1, c).

[168] *Sermo 243*, 4; PL 38, 1145.

[169] Cf. *Summa contra Gentiles* 4, 86.

[170] Ibid., 4, 88; *4 Sent.*, d. 44, q. 1, a. 3, sol. 1. The same teaching can be found in St Augustine, *De civitate Dei* 22, 15–16; CCSL 48, 834ff.

[171] Ibid.

[172] As St Augustine says, 'the bodies of the saints will rise free from any blemish or deformity, as they will be free from any corruption, burden, or impediment; their freedom of movement will be as complete as their happi-ness' (*Enchiridion* 23, 90; CCSL 46, 97).

[173] As St Augustine says, 'there will be dignity in them, not deformity, and the beauty of their virtue will shine out, a beauty in the body, yet not of the

The chief quality of the risen body will be its radiance (*claritas*).[174] In the words of Our Lord, in the resurrection the just 'will shine like the sun in the Kingdom of their Father' (cf. Mt 13:43).[175] A stream of splendour will overflow into the body from the glorified soul.[176] The radiance will exist in the soul as spiritual but in the body as bodily, 'and so in the glorious body the glory of the soul will be recognized, just as the colour of a body in a glass vase is recognized in the glass.'[177] Those of the blessed who win heroic victories over the enemies of man (the world, the flesh, and the Devil) are crowned with a special radiance known as the 'aureole' (from the Latin word meaning 'golden'). This is essentially a joy in the good works that have merited a heavenly reward, but, though existing principally in the mind, it will, 'by a certain overflow, shine also in the flesh'.[178] Fra Angelico and the iconographers of Christendom often show this aureole by a background of gold behind the figures of the blessed.

The resurrection of the dead will mean the transfiguration of the whole material order, a 'new heaven and a new earth' (cf. Is 66:22; Rev 21:1). In our altarpiece, Fra Angelico suggests this by the gleaming sea and glowing forest. This renewal of the universe is inaugurated in the bodily Resurrection of Christ. 'The world rose again in Him', says St Ambrose; 'Heaven rose again in Him, Earth rose again in Him, for there will be a new Heaven

---

body' (*De civitate Dei* 22, 19; CCSL 48, 839). Cf. St Thomas, ST 3a 54, 4, ad 1; St Bonaventure, *4 Sent.,* d. 44, 1, 31, ad 4.

[174] Cf. *4 Sent.*, d. 44, q. 2, a. 4, sol. 1.

[175] Ibid., 839.

[176] 'As then the soul in the enjoyment of the vision of God will be filled with a spiritual radiance, so by an overflow from soul to body, the body itself, in its own way, will be glad with the glory of radiance' (*Summa contra Gentiles* 4, 86; cf. ST 3a 54, 2).

[177] Cf. *4 Sent.*, d. 44, q. 2, a. 4, sol. 1.

[178] *4 Sent.*, d. 49, q. 5, a. 4, sol. 3.

and a new Earth.'[179] The Apostle teaches us that the outward form of the world is passing away (cf. 1 Cor 7:31f.); however, according to St Augustine, its nature will never pass away.[180] The material universe will be changed for the better so that it can be in harmony with the renewed body of man. As St Methodius of Olympus says, 'we who are renewed [will] dwell in a renewed world without taste of sorrow.'[181] This final regeneration will be a kind of cosmic death and resurrection, destruction followed by restoration.[182] The stars will fall from the heavens (cf. Mt 24:29), but in the end the universe will be lit up by the lamp of the Lamb (cf. Rev 21:23).

The resurrection of the dead will be the final fulfilment of creation. On the last day, when He shapes our poor flesh to be like His in glory, the Son will present the world, beautified in the Spirit, to the Father, and then God will be all in all (cf. 1 Cor 15:28). For this redemption, says St Paul, the whole material order is yearning (cf. Rom 8:22f.). It will be nature's completion and final flowering, not its rejection or replacement. Glory, like grace, fulfils nature; the re-creation presupposes and perfects creation. Every good gift that God has given us in this world will have its place, made pure and lovely, in the world of the resurrection.

---

[179] *De excessu fratris Satyri* 2, 102; PL 16, 1403A.

[180] Cf. *De civitate Dei* 20, 14; CCSL 48, 724.

[181] *Ex libro de resurrectione* 9; PG 18, 276C.

[182] According to St Maximus the Confessor, there is to be a resurrection and renewal of the whole universe (cf. *Expositio in psalmum 59*; PG 90, 857A). St Augustine says of the destruction of the universe by fire: 'In this conflagration of the world, the qualities of the corruptible elements that were appropriate for our corruptible bodies will be totally destroyed by burning, and their substance will have those qualities that are suitable, by a wonderful change, to immortal bodies. Thus the world will be made new and will be better suited to men also made new and better' (*De civitate Dei* 20, 16; CCSL 48, 727).

Conclusion
A Pastoral Theology of Beauty

Pastoral theology has to be a theology of beauty, a theological aesthetic, for, in the Catholic Church and the Orthodox Churches, pastors are themselves 'works of art'. Through the consecrating action of the Holy Spirit, God the Father fashions men to be the images of His Son, the great Shepherd of the sheep. This priestly imaging of Christ is, first of all, objective and ontological; it is rooted in the sacramental character of Holy Orders, which enables a man to act in the person and power of Christ. But the imaging of Christ must also be subjective and spiritual. The pastor who, as St Thomas says, 'bears the image of Christ' [183] in his ministry must also, by the grace of the Holy Spirit, be Christlike in his life; he must show forth the beauty of Christ in holiness.

The patrons of Fra Angelico—Pope Nicholas and Archbishop Antoninus—were men who prayed and worked for a new beauty in the Church Militant, a healing of her leprous face: [184] in restored temples but also in renovated priests, in painted icons set up above the altar, but also in ordained icons bowing low before the altar. Saintly priestly life and sacred liturgical art, the beauty of holiness and the holiness of beauty: through both, Christ, the Crown of the Saints, shines forth upon the world.

---

[183] See my article 'The Priest as Icon of Christ: A Thomist Concept', *The Priest* 50 (1994): 37–48.

[184] The image comes from Our Lord's words to St Catherine: 'Do not cease to cast before me the incense of sweet-smelling prayers for the salvation of souls, because I want to have mercy on the world, and with those prayers, sweats, and tears to wash the face of my Bride, that is, Holy Church. I have already shown her to you in the form of a maiden, her face all befouled, like a leper's' (*Dialogo*, chap. 86, 198).

II

ALTARPIECE

The San Marco altarpiece is a piece painted for the altar, an adornment of the table of Sacrifice, holy beauty for the tabernacle of the Presence. It was meant to be visible while Holy Mass was being celebrated and the Blessed Sacrament adored. Fra Angelico shows in a painting Him who on the altar is in reality present and worshipped, offered and received. Our Lady appears as the Virgin *Hodêgêtria*, the one who lights up the Way. She indicates her divine Child in the image, but she also hails Him in the Host, as if to say with John her kinsman, 'Behold the Lamb of God, behold Him who taketh away the sins of the world.'

The subject of this chapter is 'art as altarpiece'. First, again drawing chiefly on Fra Angelico's philosophical and theological sources, I shall consider art in relation to religion, to the worship of Almighty God. I shall argue that the virtue of art presupposes the virtue of religion. Secondly, I shall offer some thoughts about art in relation to the highest act of the true religion, the Eucharistic Sacrifice of Christ.

1. Art and Religion

The Modesty of Medieval Art

As a man of the Middle Ages and a son of St Thomas Aquinas, Fra Angelico had an unpretentious understanding of art. Modernism has made art seem grand and complicated, and the artist has become the Great Man, the Towering Genius. But for Fra Angelico, the business of art was more basic. St Thomas taught him that art was simply the knowledge of the right way to make things, the *recta ratio factibilium*.[1] It was an intellectual virtue, a habit of the mind, because its activity consists in imprinting an idea upon matter. More exactly, it was a virtue of the practical intellect, a knowledge, not just for contemplation and enjoyment, but for making.

In the Florence of Fra Angelico, there were as many arts as there were things to be made. The artist (*artifex*) was artisan, a workman, a maker. Painting was an art, but so was carpentry. The sculptor and the architect were artists, but so were the horseman, the physician, and the cook. This meaning did not entirely disappear from the languages of modernity. Still, in the seventeenth century, Milton calls Galileo 'the Tuscan artist', who views the moon through his 'Optic Glass . . . at evening from the top of Fesole',[2] and when Izaak Walton promises 'more directions concerning fishing', he declares, 'I would fain make you an artist.'[3]

The medieval artist had a job of work to do—for the glory of God and the good estate of the Church. He knew nothing of galleries and salons, foppish critics and fastidious collectors. As Jacques Maritain wrote in *Art and Scholasticism*:

> He did not work for society people and the dealers, but for the faithful commons; it was his mission to house their prayers, to instruct their minds, to rejoice their souls and their eyes. Matchless epoch, in which an ingenuous folk was educated in beauty without even noticing it, as perfect religious ought to pray without being aware of their prayers. . . . More

[1] Cf. ST 1a 22, 2; 1a2ae 57, 3 and 4; 93, 1; 2a2ae 47, 5.
[2] *Paradise Lost* 2, 288, in *The Works of John Milton*, vol. 2/1 (New York, 1931), 18.
[3] *The Compleat Angler*, pt. 1 (London, 1653), 125.

beautiful things were then created and there was less self-worship. The blessed humility in which the artist was situated exalted his strength and his freedom. The Renaissance was destined to drive the artist mad and make him the most miserable of men.[4]

The Virtue of Art and the Virtue of Religion

Art presupposes religion, or, rather, art presupposes the God whom religion worships. As St Thomas puts it, 'just as a work of art presupposes the work of nature, so the work of nature presupposes God.'[5] The matter with which the artist works—the stone beneath his chisel, the paint on his palette—comes from nature. His artistry depends upon its order. 'Things made by art are preserved in being by virtue of natural things, as a house is supported by the solidity of its stones.'[6] Now there is no nature without an Author of Nature, the personal and transcendent source of its being and its order. It follows, therefore, that, for St Thomas and Fra Angelico, art is a particular kind of cooperation with the Creator. The artist makes his beautiful things by following the Maker's instructions. The horseman is a true artist when he knows and acts in harmony with what God has made the horse to be. Michelangelo draws out the God-given potentialities of marble. Again to quote St Thomas: 'Things done by art and reason must be conformed to those things that are according to nature, which have been instituted by divine reason.'[7] Art in the Middle Ages is always *secundum naturam*. There is no aesthetic of perversity or disorder.

Man can be an artist because he is created in the image of the God who is the Artist of the world. This is the specifically

---

[4] Jacques Maritain, *Art and Scholasticism, with Other Essays*, new ed. (London, 1934), 22.

[5] *Summa contra Gentiles* 3, 65.

[6] Ibid.

[7] ST 2a2ae 50, 4.

Christian reinterpretation that St Thomas gives to the Aristotelian principle that 'art imitates nature.'[8] The artist cannot ignore nature, for it is the first and most marvellous poem, icon, and symphony, a measured, radiant whole, showing forth its Maker.

> The source of works of art is the human intellect, which is derived from the divine intellect, and the divine intellect is the source of all natural things. Hence not only must artistic operations imitate nature, but also works of art must imitate things that exist in nature. Thus when a master artist produces a work of art, the pupil artist is well advised to pay attention to the master's work of art, so that he can work in similar fashion. That is why the human intellect, which depends on the divine intellect for its intelligible light, must be informed concerning the things it makes by observation of things that are naturally produced, so that it may work in like manner.[9]

Art not only presupposes religion, it also bears witness to it, or, rather, it somehow bears witness to the God whom religion worships. Human art is evidence of the spirituality of the intellectual soul, and hence a pointer to the Immaterial God who created the soul in His image. In man's heart there is a restless longing for truth and beauty, for order and harmony, that the satisfaction of the sense appetites cannot quench. In his joy in beauty, whether in nature or art, man receives confirmation of the spiritual dignity of his intellect. The enjoyment of beauty is always a meeting of minds. As Jacques Maritain says:

> The intelligence delights in the beautiful because in the beautiful it finds itself again and recognizes itself, and makes contact with its own light. This is so true that those—such as Saint Francis of Assisi—perceive and savour more the beauty of things who know that things come forth from an intelligence, and who relate them to their author.[10]

[8] *Sententia super Physicam*, lib. 2, lect. 4, no. 6.
[9] *Sententia libri Politicorum*, lib. 1, lect. 1.
[10] Maritain, *Art and Scholasticism*, 25.

If man's art points to God, God's art, the beauty of the natural world, proclaims Him. According to St Thomas and St Bonaventure, following St Augustine, all things carry the trace (*vestigium*) of their Triune Creator and thus of His beauty.[11] (Rational creatures, of course, are made to His image.) The loveliness of heaven and earth tells the glory of God. The stars of the sky, the mountains and hills, the green things upon the earth are truly beautiful, and yet, being changeable, they cannot be the artisans of their own loveliness. 'They cry aloud', says St Augustine, 'that they did not make themselves.'[12] They are beautiful because God is beautiful, though they are not beautiful as He is beautiful; compared with Him, they are not beautiful.[13] Their beauty is their voice. We can hear and question it:

> Question the beauty of the earth, question the beauty of the sea, question the beauty of the air distending and diffusing itself, question the beauty of the sky. . . . Question all these things. All respond: 'See, we are beautiful.' Their beauty is a confession. These beauties are subject to change. Who made them if not the Beautiful One who is not subject to change?[14]

According to St Bonaventure, this truth of the dogma of creation was the foundation of St Francis's love of all creatures.

> In beautiful things he saw Supreme Beauty Himself and through His traces (*vestigia*) imprinted on creation 'he followed His Beloved' (cf. Job 23:11) everywhere, making from all things a ladder by which he could climb up and embrace Him who is 'utterly desirable' (cf. Song 5:16).[15]

For St Thomas, religion is the virtue that renders due honour to God, One and Triune, the God of infinite beauty.[16] If a man

[11] See chap. 1, pp. 52ff.

[12] *Confessiones* 11, 4, 6; CCSL 27, 197.

[13] Ibid.

[14] *Sermo 241*, 2; PL 38, 1134.

[15] *Legenda Sancti Francisci*, cap. 9, no. 1; *Sancti Bonaventurae opera omnia*, vol. 8 (Quaracchi, 1898), 530.

[16] Cf. ST 2a2ae 81, 2 and 5. On the Trinitarian dimension, the worship of the Three Persons in God, see 2a2ae 81, 3, ad 1; 84, 1, ad 3; 3a 25, 1, ad 1.

does not exercise that virtue, at least to the extent of recognizing the order of God's creation, he is incapable of art. An atheistic art is a self-contradiction. Human making has no meaning if there is no divine Maker to give man meaning. If there is no God, there is no truth, beauty, or goodness; nature has no order or harmony, and art has no foundation. There can be no culture without cult, without worship, the first act of the virtue of religion. As Balthasar says:

> All great art is religious, an act of homage before the glory of what exists. Where the religious dimension disappears, the homage degenerates into something that is merely attractive and pleasing; where the glorious disappears, we are left with what is usually called the 'beautiful'.[17]

Not every artist has been religious in the sense of being a believer who formally worships the one true God, but all great art has been religious in the sense that it manifests the wonder of being, the beauty of things as they reflect the brilliance of the divine Wisdom that made them. Balthasar says of the very first works of literary art in the West, the *Iliad* and *Odyssey*: 'In no other poetry of world literature does the thought of God occur so often . . . the thought of His power, His presence, His working in everything, through external events, through inner inspiration and the endowing with strength.'[18] The denial of God destroys art's foundations. As George Steiner wrote some years ago in his book *Real Presences*:

> What I affirm is the intuition that where God's presence is no longer a tenable supposition, and where His absence is no longer a felt, indeed overbearing weight, certain dimensions of thought and creativity are no longer attainable.[19]

---

[17] H 3/1/1, 14; GL 4, 12f.

[18] Ibid., 48; GL 4, 49.

[19] George Steiner, *Real Presences* (London, 1990), 229. Chateaubriand likewise argues that 'unbelief is the principal cause of the decadence of taste and genius' (*Génie du christianisme*, in *Oeuvres complètes*, vol. 16 [Paris, 1836], 4).

To create, according to St Thomas, is to give being, to make something out of nothing. Therefore, creation is the proper act of God alone, of Him Who Is, whose very essence is to be.[20] The artist cannot, therefore, in the strict sense be creative.[21] He does not produce things out of nothing but reshapes what already exists. The nearest any man comes to creating is in procreation, but here, too, the secondary causality of the creature is entirely dependent on the primary causality of the Creator. Parents are parents of the whole person of their child, and yet they prepare only the matter, which is united to a spiritual soul created immediately out of nothing by God. Their role is precisely *pro*-creation, cooperation with the Creator in the transmission of human life. Parents do not, strictly speaking, 'create' their children; they receive them from God as His gift and the fruit of their love. That is one of the reasons why the Catholic Church condemns all techniques of *in vitro* fertilization as gravely sinful: they divorce life from love and make the child appear like a product rather than a person.[22]

Some art is directly ordered to the glorification of God and the sanctification of man.[23] If this ordering to religion is what the Schoolmen call the *finis operis*, the purpose of the work of art itself, then the art is *sacred art*, liturgical art: for example, the paintings of Andrei Rublev and Fra Angelico, the Masses of Byrd and Palestrina, and the hymns of St John Damascene and

[20] Cf. ST 1a 45, 5.

[21] Fr Bertrand de Margerie, S.J., writes: 'The worker can only act by means of a body, a mind, a freedom that he did not give himself but that come from the one and only Creator; and his work does not give *being*, but only a new *configuration* to the real. . . . A salutary and exciting humiliation: it is precisely by this dependent and conditioned work that my finite and contingent being can collaborate with the one and only, absolute Creator in the fulfilment of the universe and so be saved eternally' (*Les perfections du Dieu de Jésus Christ* [Paris, 1981], 183f.).

[22] See CCC 2373ff.; Congregation for the Doctrine of the Faith, *Donum vitae* (February 22, 1987), passim.

[23] Cf. *Sacrosanctum concilium*, no. 112, on sacred music.

St Thomas Aquinas. This kind of art has been defined very beautifully by the *Catechism of the Catholic Church*:

> *Sacred art* is true and beautiful when its form corresponds to its particular vocation: evoking and glorifying, in faith and adoration, the transcendent mystery of God—the surpassing invisible beauty of truth and love visible in Christ, who 'reflects the glory of God and bears the very stamp of his nature' (cf. Heb 1:3), in whom 'the whole fullness of deity dwells bodily' (cf. Col 2:9). This spiritual beauty of God is reflected in the most holy Virgin Mother of God, the angels, and saints. Genuine sacred art draws man to adoration, to prayer, and to the love of God, Creator and Savior, the Holy One and Sanctifier.[24]

In other cases, the ordering of the art to the glory of God is the end of the artist, the *finis operantis*. In other words, his motive is to glorify God, even though the work of art itself is not destined for the beautification of church and liturgy. This is *religious art*, art shaped and pervaded by faith and prayer. Examples here would be the painting of Rouault, the music of Messiaen, and the poetry of St John of the Cross, George Herbert, and Gerard Manley Hopkins.

The great French Catholic poet and dramatist Paul Claudel argued that great art, even when it is not explicitly religious, can achieve good spiritual effects in others, if not in the artist himself. He gives as an example the poetry of Rimbaud. Its haunting beauty, its sense of eternity and the transcendent mystery of human life, helped to liberate Claudel from the positivistic scepticism of his youth—the sickening servile worship of science to be found in Ernest Renan.

> I shall always remember that morning in June 1886 when I bought the little copy of *Vogue* containing the first part of *Illuminations*. It really was an illumination for me. At last I came out of that hideous world of Taine, of Renan and the other Molochs

[24] CCC 2502.

of the nineteenth century, that penal colony, that appalling machine governed by laws that were completely inflexible and,
horror of horrors, knowable and teachable. . . . I had the revelation of the supernatural.[25]

Positivism, materialism, atheism—these are the deadly enemies of art, for they blind a man to the wealth and wonder of
being. It was from all such rude reductions of reality that William Blake asked to be delivered when he prayed, 'May God us
keep/ From single vision and Newton's sleep.'[26] For a Comte
or a Marx, for a Renan or a Taine, the world is a machine, a
closed system. But the great artists, even when they lack ex-
plicit faith, reveal the marvel of what is, in all its transcendental
richness. The lovely Muse of Poetry may not always be a
Christian, but, as Gertrud von Le Fort suggested, 'in her deep-
est impulses, unconsciously yet irresistibly, [she is] ordered towards what is Christian and is flooded with a gentle Advent-like
light.'[27]

Art and Morality

Art is a virtue, but, according to St Thomas, it is not the kind of
virtue that makes men good; its goal is the good of the thing
made rather than the good of the maker. More precisely, art
makes the artist capable of making the right judgement about
how to make a good work of art: 'Perfectio artis consistit in

[25] Jacques Rivière and Paul Claudel, *Correspondance 1907–1914* (Paris, 1926),
142f. Newman said something similar about the influence of Sir Walter Scott's
literary art on the Oxford Movement: he helped to 'prepare men for some
closer and more practical approximation to Catholic truth' ('Prospects of the
Anglican Church', in *Essays and Sketches*, vol. 1, new ed. [New York, 1948],
337).

[26] Letter to Thomas Butts (November 22, 1802); *Selected Poetry and Prose of
William Blake* (New York, 1953), 420.

[27] Gertrud von Le Fort, 'Vom Wesen christlicher Dichtung', in *Aufzeich-
nungen und Erinnerungen* (Zurich, 1958), 47.

iudicando.'[28] Its aim is to make a good work of art, not to make the willing of that work of art good. According to St Thomas, it is the *finis operis* with which the virtue of art is concerned, not the *finis operantis*. As Father Bede Jarrett, O.P., wrote in his *Social Theories of the Middle Ages*:

> It was the thing and not the man that was the measurement of art, and purpose affected the thing while motive affected the man. The purpose, therefore, was to be scrutinized, never the motive. For example, there could be no art in making an idol to be worshipped, for right reason could not approve the purpose of the thing.[29]

We commend the craftsman, not for the will with which he works, but for the quality of the work he actually produces.[30] Art is, therefore, an imperfect, an incomplete virtue.[31]

St Thomas contrasts art with prudence; in fact, he delights in getting these two virtues to dance and show off their likenesses and unlikenesses. To quote Father Jarrett again: 'His style is enlivened when he comes to treat of it. Epigrams break from his pen when he writes of it or refers to it.'[32] Art deals with the right way to *make* things; its actions pass into external matter—painting, sawing, carving. By contrast, prudence is about the right way to *do* things, how to behave as a human being; its actions remain rooted within the moral field of the agent—his seeing and hearing, his thinking and willing. Art is for the good of the work, while prudence is for the good of the worker. Prudence, then, unlike art, depends on the goodness of the will, because it is the will that chooses the goal of human actions. It is a perfect virtue. It perfects a man as a man. In art, reason aims at

---

[28] ST 2a2ae 47, 8.
[29] Bede Jarrett, O.P., *Social Theories of the Middle Ages, 1200–1500* (London, 1926), 239.
[30] Cf. ST 1a2ae 57, 3.
[31] Ibid., ad 1.
[32] Jarrett, *Social Theories*, 239.

a particular goal, but in morality, reason aims at the universal goal of all human life. An artist can sin, miss the mark, in two ways: first, by failing to achieve his artistic goal; secondly, by producing something bad in order to deceive others. In the first case, he sins as an artist; in the second, as a man.[33] To deploy his art well, he needs the moral virtues. The virtue of art gives a man the capacity to do good work, but it does not ensure that he uses his art well—for that he needs the moral virtues that perfect his appetites. Thus it would seem that the capacity to produce good works of art is independent of one's moral or spiritual condition.

This conclusion shocks us. It seems as if St Thomas is divorcing art from morality, undermining our effort to see a connection between the sensible loveliness of Fra Angelico's paintings and the spiritual loveliness of his life. Not really. Like all the philosophers and artists of the Middle Ages, St Thomas has his eyes fixed on the work rather than the worker: it is the thing made that counts. He cannot deny the possibility, the actuality, of a masterpiece being made by a miscreant. However, it is possible to argue from a strictly Thomistic starting point that 'the morally good person, all other things being equal, will be a better artist.'[34] The moral virtues, while retaining their orientation towards the end of man, can also further the ends of art.

Let us consider the case of an artist in the state of grace, in whom the moral virtues are shaped by charity. His life of supernatural virtue is not the source of his art, but it can transfigure it. Art has its beginning in seeing, in what Josef Pieper calls 'contemplation'[35]

---

[33] Cf. ST 1a2ae 21, 2, ad 2.

[34] Ralph McInerny, *Art and Prudence: Studies in the Thought of Jacques Maritain* (Notre Dame, 1988), 171.

[35] 'Music, the fine arts, poetry—anything that festively raises up human existence and thereby constitutes its true riches—all derive their life from a hidden root, and this root is a contemplation which is turned toward God and the world so as to affirm them' (*Only the Lover Sings: Art and Contemplation* [San Francisco, 1990], 11). In another book, Pieper goes on to argue that this

and Maritain 'creative intuition'.[36] Now eyes see better in the light of love. *Ubi amor, ibi oculus*. Charity, the supernatural love of God and neighbour that perfects the will, refines and elevates the natural seeing of the mind. The self-absorbed man will glimpse nothing but reflections of himself in the waters of reality, but the self-giving man, the man taken out of himself and plunged into the charity of the Trinity, will let things have their own light and delight. A man without the spiritual beauty of temperance will be too blinded by his passions to perceive the many-splendoured thing; he will tend, for example, to see the body, not as a sacrament, the expressive incarnation of the spiritual soul and thus of the person, but as a machine for obtaining pleasure.[37] By contrast, the pure in heart will have eyes that are clear and unclouded. The poet must gaze on God's world with wonder and humility. He must be, or become again, a little child. The man of the world, who has 'seen and done it all' and lost his capacity for hope and surprise, cannot be a poet. Or rather, to be a poet, he must first be reborn. The emptiness of experience must be filled up with the richness of restored innocence. As Charles Péguy says:

natural contemplation is an attitude of wonder, the sense that 'each and every thing holds and hides, in its depths, a sign of its divine origin. To see this is to see that this thing and all things are good, beyond all understanding. You see it, and you are happy. This is the entire doctrine of the contemplation of earthly things' (*Philosophie, Kontemplation, Weisheit* [Einsiedeln, 1991], 18).

[36] Maritain writes: 'In the mind of the poet, poetic knowledge arises in an unconscious or preconscious manner, and emerges into consciousness in a sometimes almost imperceptible though imperative and irrefragable way, through an impact both emotional and intellectual or through an unpredictable experiential insight, which gives notice of its existence, but does not express it' (*Creative Intuition in Art and Poetry* [New York, 1953], 118).

[37] Julien Green says of the Renaissance in contrast to that final flowering of the Gothic in the so-called 'Primitives': 'The great Paradise of Fra Angelico, lost by the Renaissance, which could offer us only a replacement Paradise— *entirely carnal*' (*Journal*, November 17, 1968, in *Oeuvres complètes* [Paris, 1977], 493).

They say they're full of experience; they gain from
    experience.
[D]ay by day they pile up their experience.
    'Some treasure!', says God.
A treasure of emptiness and of dearth . . .
A treasure of wrinkles and worries.
The treasure of the lean years . . .
What you call experience, your experience, I call
    dissipation, diminishment, decrease, the loss of
    innocence.
It's a perpetual degradation.
No, it is innocence that is full and experience that is
    empty.
It is innocence that wins and experience that loses.
It is innocence that is young and experience that is old.
It is innocence that increases and experience that
    decreases.
It is innocence that is born and experience that dies.
It is innocence that knows and experience that does
    not know.
It is the child who is full and the man who is empty.
Like an empty gourd, like an empty beer-barrel.
So, then, says God, that's what I think of your
    'experience'.[38]

The argument for art's dependence on the clarity of moral
vision has never been presented more eloquently than by Cardinal Newman in one of his early essays:

> We do not hesitate to say that poetry is ultimately founded on
> correct moral perception. . . . Of course . . . we do not mean to
> imply that a poet must necessarily display virtuous and religious

---

[38] Charles Péguy, 'Le Mystère des Saints Innocents', in *Oeuvres poétiques
complètes* (Paris, 1957), 787f.

feeling; we are not speaking of the actual material of poetry, but of its sources. A right moral state of heart is the formal and scientific condition of a poetical mind. . . . As motives short of the purest lead to actions intrinsically less good, so frames of mind short of virtuous will produce a partial and limited poetry. . . . [A] right moral feeling places the mind in the very centre of that circle from which all the rays have their origin and range; whereas minds otherwise placed command but a portion of the whole circuit of poetry.[39]

Art and Sanctity

The holiness of beauty is ordered to the beauty of holiness. Sacred art is intended to encourage saintly life. Both are transparent to Christ, radiate the splendour of His truth. Both, in their different ways, are gifts of God. Aristotle speaks of a gift for finding metaphors, a gift inborn, not something acquired.[40] Using a familiar distinction of Scholastic theology, Claudel suggests that artistic genius should be seen as an example of *gratia gratis data*, a charism, an extraordinary gift given to certain men not in the first place for their own benefit but for that of others. This is, he says, the grace 'that makes poets, Arthur Rimbaud, for example', by contrast with Sanctifying Grace, *gratia gratum faciens*, the grace that makes us pleasing to God, the grace 'that makes saints'.[41]

It is Christ who makes saints, not art. More precisely, to use the distinctions of Thomistic theology, it is the Triune Godhead that is the principal efficient cause of our sanctification and the humanity of Christ the instrumental cause. In other words, the Father pours out a share of His divine life in the Holy Spirit through the instrumentality of the glorified manhood of the

[39] 'Poetry, with reference to Aristotle's *Poetics*', in *Essays and Sketches*, 1: 74f.
[40] *Poetics* 1459a5.
[41] 'La Poésie est un art', in *Oeuvres complètes de Paul Claudel*, vol. 18, *Accompagnements, discours et remerciements* (Paris, 1961), 19.

Son. This grace flows, by the divine will of the Trinity and the human will of the Son, into the Sacraments of the Church, which sanctify us *ex opere operato*, through the power of the completed rite, or, rather, through the efficacy of the Eternal High Priest acting in and through His Church. Art does not and cannot sanctify us in this way. It is not a Sacrament. However, Christian art can be regarded as an example of what the Catholic Church calls a 'sacramental', something that sanctifies *ex opere operantis*, through the intercession of the Church and the devotion of her members.[42] The Holy Spirit, through the work of art, can move us back to God or forward in our following of Christ. As St John Damascene says, 'the beauty of the images moves me to contemplation, as a meadow delights the eyes and subtly infuses the soul with the glory of God.'[43] St Teresa of Avila was converted to a more fervent practice of prayer and the evangelical counsels through an image of the Suffering Christ, the *Ecce Homo*.[44] The 'little Thérèse' of Lisieux was healed through the miraculous image of the Virgin of the Smile.[45] Like his father St Dominic, St Thomas Aquinas preferred to pray before a crucifix, through which, on several occasions, Our Lord spoke directly to him. He commends the devotion in his exposition of the Apostles' Creed: 'If you seek an example of humility, look on the Crucified.'[46] Julien Green says of the Brancacci

[42] 'Holy Mother Church has, moreover, instituted sacramentals. These are sacred signs which bear a resemblance to the sacraments. They signify effects, particularly of a spiritual nature, which are obtained through the intercession of the Church. By them men are disposed to receive the chief effect of the sacraments, and various occasions in life are rendered holy' (CCC 1667, quoting the Second Vatican Council, *Sacrosanctum concilium*, no. 60).

[43] *De imaginibus* 1, 27; PG 94, 1268AB.

[44] 'Era de Cristo muy llagado', *Libro de la Vida*, chap. 9; *Obras de Sta Teresa de Jesus*, ed. P. Silverio de Sta Teresa, vol. 1 (Burgos, 1915), 63; ET, *The Complete Works of St Teresa of Jesus*, vol. 1 (London, 1946), 54.

[45] Saint Thérèse de l'Enfant-Jésus et de la Saint-Face, *Histoire d'une âme: Manuscrits autobiographiques* (Paris, 1972), 79ff.

[46] *In Symbolum Apostolorum*, a. 4.

chapel at Santa Maria del Carmine that 'no sermon was more persuasive, more urgent, than these figures on the walls . . . the gravity of St Peter, the wonderful serenity of the Saviour. *You cannot see it and stay the same.*'[47]

If holy beauty can excite the beauty of holiness, the beauty of holiness certainly encourages holy beauty. As Pope John Paul II has said:

> [T]hrough the light that they emanate, through their interior freedom, through the power of their personality, [the saints] have marked the artistic thought and expression of entire periods of our history. It is enough to mention St Francis of Assisi. He had a poet's temperament, which is amply confirmed by his words, his attitude, his innate sense of the symbolic gesture. Although he was far from being involved in any literary concern, he was nevertheless the creator of a new culture, in the areas of artistic thought and expression. A St Bonaventure or a Giotto could not have developed had it not been for him.[48]

During the Dark Ages, the cult of the saints—the stories of their lives and miracles, the veneration of their relics, and the invoking of their prayers—had a transfiguring effect on the culture of the Barbarians of the West. As Christopher Dawson says of the hagiography of Gregory of Tours (c. 540–594):

> This literature and the cult to which it corresponds represent the other side of the dark picture of contemporary society which he presents in his *History of the Franks*. On the one side, we see a world of violence and injustice which is sinking to destruction by its own weight. But on the other side there is the world of divine power and mystery in which the harsh necessities of daily experience no longer dominate life—where nothing is impossible and every human suffering and misfortune may find a remedy.[49]

---

[47] *Journal*, November 17, 1968, in *Oeuvres complètes* (Paris, 1977), 493.

[48] Address of March 18, 1994.

[49] C. Dawson, *Religion and the Rise of Western Culture*, new ed. (New York, 1958), 34.

The Son of God became man in order to elevate and rebeautify our fallen race. This beauty He bestows in the Sacraments of the Church. In the saints, the Barbarians found men and women truly transfigured in Christ's beauty.

St Francis of Assisi had a similar effect on the arts, on the whole culture, of Europe. Through Cimabue and Giotto, Francis brought the gift of tears into Western painting. In the *laudi* of his spiritual son Jacopone da Todi, and in his own *Canticle* (with which vernacular literature in Italy begins), he purified and surrendered to the Trinity the gaiety of the troubadours. As Francis Thompson said, 'sworn to Poverty he forswore not Beauty, but discerned through the lamp Beauty the Light God. . . . Poetry clung round the cowls of his Order.'[50] The Franciscan artists prolong the mission of their father Francis: they present the joyful, sorrowful, and glorious mysteries of Christ for adoration, imitation, and participation by the Christian. Through Francis and all the saints, the radiance of the Virgin's Child frees men's minds and heals their imaginations. Tongues are unlocked. Unsuspected horizons of beauty attract the eye.

Art and Poverty

It is the consistent teaching of the saints that adornment is for the house and worship of God, not for the homes and persons of the priests of God. By a strange irony, the Iconoclastic clergy of the eighth century were notorious fops and dandies: the men who smashed the holy icons smeared themselves with scent. That is why the sixteenth canon of the Second Council of Nicaea (787) ruled 'that it does not become those in holy orders to be clad in costly apparel'.[51] St Francis robed himself in rags

[50] 'Shelley', in *The Complete Works of Francis Thompson*, new ed., vol. 3 (Westmin ster, 1947), 2.

[51] Theodore Balsamon et al., *In canones SS. Apostolorum, Conciliorum et in epistolas canonicas SS. Patrum commentaria*; PG 137, 968C–972C.

but believed that nothing but the best should adorn the altar of the Lord.[52] 'O worship the Lord in the beauty of holiness': the beauty of holy art in the sanctuary, the beauty of holy poverty in the priest. St Catherine later condemns those incontinent priests who embellish their own accommodations with what, 'out of reverence for the Blood', ought to beautify the Church and her temples.[53]

Art and the Creed: The Trinity

The dogmas of the Church's faith are not only the subject matter of her art but the condition of its possibility. The beauty of Christian art—the icon, the hymn of praise—flows directly from the truth of Christian Revelation. St Irenaeus sees God the Father as the divine Artist fashioning the world's beauty out of nothing by His hands, the Son, and the Spirit.[54] The first poem is the cosmos, written with His own hands by God. The almighty Father created all things through His Son-Word and in their Spirit-Love, and so all things sing of the Trinity's glory. The analogy is developed by St Augustine, who adds that the eternal Word is the 'Art' of the Father,[55] the brilliant Wisdom through whom the Father conceives and accomplishes His wonders, the pattern of all possible beauty. In knowing Himself in His Son, the Father knows all the ways in which His infinite perfections can be mirrored by creatures. The consubstantial Word is, there-

[52] Cf. his 'Letter to All Clerics', in *St Francis of Assisi: Omnibus of Sources*, new ed. (Quincy, 1991), 101.

[53] Cf. *Dialogo della divina provvidenza*, chap. 123, ed. G. Cavallini (Rome, 1968), 309.

[54] Cf. *Adversus haereses* 4, *praefatio* 4; PG 7, 975B.

[55] St Augustine speaks of 'ars quaedam omnipotentis Dei' (*De Trinitate* 5, 10, 11; CCSL 50, 241). St Bonaventure adds the important, anti-Arian gloss: the Son proceeds from the Father (by way of generation) 'as the art of reason and of making works of art, not as Himself a work of art' (*1 Sent.*, d. 10, a. 1, q. 1, concl. 3; *Sancti Bonaventurae opera omnia*, vol. 1 (Quaracchi, 1892), 196).

fore, the uncreated model of all creatures. As St Thomas explains:

> If someone makes something, he has to preconceive it in wisdom, which is the form and pattern of the thing made. The form conceived beforehand in the mind of the craftsman is the pattern of the chest to be made. So God does nothing except through the concept of His intellect, which is His Wisdom conceived from eternity, namely, the Word of God, the Son of God. And so it is impossible that He does anything except through the Son.[56]

The Father makes His beautiful works of art not only through the Art that is the Son but also in the Love that is the Holy Spirit.[57] Creatures are thus not only words of the Word but also gifts of the Gift, of Him who is the mutual Gift of the Father and the Son. As St Thomas says in the first question on creation in the First Part of the *Summa Theologiae*:

> God is the cause of things by His intellect and will, just as the artist is the cause of the things made by his art. Now the artist works through the word conceived in his intellect and by the love of his will for something. So, too, God the Father made the creature through His Word, who is His Son, and through His Love, which is the Holy Spirit. And so the processions of the Persons are the model of the processions of creatures inasmuch as they include the essential attributes, namely, knowledge and will.[58]

St Thomas bids us meditate on the works of God's creation because it will strengthen our faith; it will enhance our sense of wonder at the brilliance of the Wisdom, the Word and Art, through whom the Father in His Love made them all:

[56] *Lectura super Ioannem*, cap. 1, lect. 2.

[57] St Thomas compares the Spirit of Love, in whom the Father through His Son-Wisdom creates all things, to the 'pleasure' (*complacentia*) an artist takes in his art (cf. ST 1a 74, 3, ad 3).

[58] ST 1a 45, 6.

Works of art illustrate the art itself, because they bear the im-
print of that art. Now God brought things into being by His
Wisdom. . . . Hence we are able to gather the Wisdom of God
from the consideration of His works, since by a kind of commu-
nication of His likeness it is spread abroad in the things He has
made.[59]

Nature, says Dante, 'takes her course from the Sublime Intellect and Its Art'. Human art must, therefore, follow Nature, 'like
a pupil with his master', and 'we may call/ This art of yours
God's grandchild, as it were.' Human art, through nature, descends from the almighty Art of the Father.[60]

Art and the Creed: The Incarnation

The Incarnation brought a new beauty into the world; it
brought Divine Beauty, the Son and Splendour of the Father,
into human nature, into the womb of the Virgin. The union of
humanity with divinity in the hypostasis of the Word is the elevation of everything human—including human art. The Art of
the Father enters into His own handiwork to transfigure it from
within. If the world is beautiful through its creation, it is raised
to a dignity beyond compare through its re-creation in Christ.
In God the Word, incarnate from the Virgin Mary, crucified and
risen in the flesh, the Eucharistic Lord of the Church, the cosmic poem finds its fullest meaning, its beginning and its end.

The divine Art awakens human art. 'God's Word', says Balthasar, 'did not come to rob us of speech but to untie our
tongues in a manner hitherto unknown.'[61] Poetry is reborn, and

---

[59] Ibid., 2a2ae 2, 2.

[60] *Inferno* 11, 97ff.; *Dantis Aligherii Divina Comoedia edita mandatu Pauli VI
Pont. Max.* (Vatican City, 1965), 69f.; ET, *The Comedy of Dante Alighieri, the
Florentine*, trans. Dorothy L. Sayers (Baltimore, 1949), 136f.

[61] Hans Urs von Balthasar, introduction to Peter Baumhauer, *Am Ufer des
Zeitlands: Gedichte* (Einsiedeln, 1985), 11.

painting receives a new charter. As the 'Iconodule' Fathers of the eighth and ninth centuries teach us, without ceasing to be invisible and uncircumscribable in His divine nature, the eternal Son has assumed a complete and concrete human nature into the unity of His Person, and in that human nature He is visible, circumscribable, capable of representation in art. We have seen Him with our eyes and touched Him with our hands (cf. 1 Jn 1:1f.). God the Son has the face and features of a man. St Gregory II, the great Iconodule Pope of the early eighth century, argued that if there had been no Incarnation, there could be no icons, but since there has been an Incarnation, there *must* be icons:

> If the Lord is not incarnate, then His holy image, according to the flesh, should not be painted. If He was not born in Bethlehem of the glorious Virgin Mother of God, if the Magi did not bring Him gifts . . . , if He did not accomplish things beyond expectation, then such things should never be painted. . . . But if all these things have been accomplished, . . . I would, were it possible, that the heavens, earth, and sea, every animal, plant, all other creatures, should publish them abroad by words, by writing, or by pictures.[62]

The Incarnation showers a second spring upon the material world. According to the Fathers, the Iconoclastic rejection betrayed a low and unchristian view of matter. The totality of the material creation has been touched, and is thus objectively and in principle transfigured, by God the Son's taking of flesh from the Virgin and His rising in the flesh from the tomb. Material substances, which already by their very being show forth the beauty of the Creator, attain a new transparency to Him through His personal entry into the bodily realm. St John Damascene, one of the great defenders of the holy icons and an important source for the Christology of St Thomas, argued as follows:

[62] Mansi 13, 96AC.

> I do not worship matter, I worship the God of matter, who became matter for my sake, and deigned to inhabit matter, who worked out my salvation through matter. I will not cease from honouring that matter which works my salvation.[63]

In making and venerating icons, man reveals his own iconic dignity as God's creature. Made in the image of the Triune God, he is called to be priest of the cosmos, giving free and rational voice to the nonrational creation's objective praising of the Creator. In Adam man failed in that vocation, but in Christ he regains it. In sacred art he takes the good things of this earth, newly charged with glory through the Incarnation and Resurrection, and shapes them into a visual canticle of worship.

2. Art and the Eucharist

A Presence beyond All Art

In the Holy Eucharist there is a presence beyond all human art. The Iconoclasts would not venerate the holy icons because, so they said, the Eucharist is the only acceptable icon of Christ. The Second Council of Nicaea dismissed this sophistry with the wave of a hand: 'Neither the Lord nor the Apostles nor the Fathers ever called the unbloody Sacrifice offered up by priests an "image" but rather "true Body" and "true Blood".'[64] The Sacred Host is not a mere icon or figure, but the true Body of Christ really, truly, and substantially present under the appearances of bread. However highly they cherish the holy images, the Fathers of Nicaea II subordinate them to Christ's infinitely

---

[63] *De imaginibus* I, 16; PG 94, 1245AB.

[64] Mansi 13, 265B. This text was cited by the theologians of the Council of Trent in defence of Catholic teaching on both the Real Presence and the Eucharistic Sacrifice (cf. *Concilium Tridentinum*, tom. 6/3, ed. T. Freudenberger [Freiburg im Breisgau, 1974], 8, lines 16ff.; 391, lines 15ff.).

greater gift to us of His Body, Blood, Soul, and Divinity in the life-giving mysteries of the altar.

In the Eucharist there is a beauty, a hidden loveliness, beyond the beauty of all art. The Lamb of God comes to the altar of His Bride in the glory of the Father and the Holy Spirit, invisibly escorted by the angels. Only humble accidents veil the radiance of His flesh. Christ is beauty, and He becomes present to make us beautiful. This dogmatic truth has fired the minds and imaginations of Christian artists for two thousand years. Most of the great art of the West has been, directly or indirectly, an 'altarpiece'. In 1994, in an address to the Pontifical Council for Culture, Pope John Paul II said that not only was Christianity 'the creator of culture in its very foundation', 'the very concept of beauty in ancient Europe is largely the result of the Christian culture of its peoples, and its landscape reflects this inspiration.'[65] The Holy Father went on to say that Europe's patrimony of beauty has at its centre, its living heart, the Most Blessed Sacrament of the Altar.

> The cathedrals, the humble country churches, the religious music, architecture, sculpture, and painting all radiate the mystery of the *verum Corpus, natum de Maria Virgine*, towards which everything converges in a movement of wonder.[66]

Pope John Paul cites the figure of Palestrina. After the cataclysmic events of the sixteenth century, the eruption of the Protestant Reformation and the destruction it unleashed, the Church regained in Palestrina, who was closely associated with St Philip Neri, 'a voice made peaceful through contemplation of the Eucharistic mystery, like the calm breathing of a soul that knows that it is loved by God'.[67] Chesterton once said of Ruskin that he 'seemed to want all parts of the Cathedral except the altar'.[68]

---

[65] Address of March 18, 1994.
[66] Ibid.
[67] Ibid.
[68] G. K. Chesterton, *The Victorian Age in Literature* (London, 1913), 65.

It must be said that, if that judgment be true, then however much Ruskin knew about the cathedrals of the Middle Ages, he did not understand them at all.

The holy beauty of medieval Durham was intended to honour St Cuthbert, but in the first place it was meant to glorify St Cuthbert's Eucharistic Lord. Even in death, Durham's patron pointed beyond himself to the Holy Sacrifice of the Mass. In 1104, when the tomb of St Cuthbert was opened, his body was found to be not only incorrupt but still bearing the material necessities for the celebration of Mass: a corporal, a chalice and paten, and a silver portable altar. In ceremonial and iconography, the Catholic cathedral of Durham was filled with loveliness to laud Sion's Shepherd and King. In 1217 the Council of Durham, which was probably the first local council after Lateran IV to speak of Transubstantiation, decreed that the Blessed Sacrament was to be reserved in a 'clean and locked pyx'.[69] And so it was, in the cathedral and throughout the diocese.

There were many beautiful acts of Eucharistic adoration in Catholic Durham. *The Rites of Durham* informs us that, on Easter Sunday morning, between three and four o'clock, two of the oldest monks came to the Easter Sepulchre, 'being set up upon Good Friday after the Passion all covered with red velvet and embroidered with gold'. They knelt before the Blessed Sacrament, which had been reserved there since Good Friday, and censed It with a pair of silver censers.

> [T]hen they both rising came to the sepulchre, out of the which with great reverence they took a marvellous beautiful image of Our Saviour representing the Resurrection with a Cross in His hand, in the breast whereof was enclosed in bright most pure crystal the Holy Sacrament of the Altar, through the which crystal the Blessed Host was conspicuous to the beholders, then after the elevation of the said picture carried by the said two

[69] Mansi 22, 1118, 1119.

monks upon a fair velvet cushion all embroidered singing the
anthem of *Christus Resurgens*.[70]

At last, they brought the Christ-bearing image of Christ to
the High Altar, and there It stayed until Ascension Day.[71] By
their senses, the monks of Durham could not see the risen body
of Christ in its beauty, but by chant and procession, by incense
and images, their faith in its Real Presence was strengthened.

The beauty of all the arts is indebted to the holiness of the
Mass, even the art of theatre.[72] The plays of a Shakespeare or a
Claudel have their remote preparation in the dramatic dialogues
that, from the tenth century, begin to appear in the Masses of
Christmas Day and Easter Sunday. The procession of the Blessed
Sacrament on the feast of Corpus Christi became a kind of
drama festival throughout medieval Europe: through wooden
figures and tableaux, by pageants and mystery plays, the whole
history of salvation from Genesis to the Apocalypse was acted
out before the People of God. This had a sound foundation in
Eucharistic dogma. In the Mass, Christ's Sacrifice on the Cross is
more than merely recalled: it is re-presented, the 'theodrama' of
Calvary is reenacted, and its saving power is applied to the living
and the dead. In the seventeenth century, Calderon is still writing *autos sacramentales*,[73] theatrical unfoldings of the drama of the

[70] *Rites of Durham: Being a Description or Brief Declaration of all the Ancient
Monuments, Rites and Customs Belonging or Being within the Monastical Church of
Durham before the Suppression*, Surtees Society, no. 107 (1903), 107.

[71] Ibid., 12f.

[72] See Lynette R. Muir, *The Biblical Drama of Medieval Europe* (Cambridge,
1995), 13, 16, 24ff.

[73] '*Autos sacramentales* are dramatic one-act plays in praise of the Sacrament
of the Eucharist (the Real Presence of Jesus Christ in the consecrated Host).
. . . They have, therefore, a sacred and allegorical character. They were performed in the town square, on the afternoon of Corpus Christi and for several
afternoons following. It was [Calderon] who wrote the greatest number of
autos and, combining the symbolism with the theatrical necessities, gave them
their most perfect form' (M. Romera-Navarro, *Historia de la literatura española*
[New York, 1928], 384).

Mass. Of *The Great Theatre of the World*, Balthasar says: 'Everything is founded on an unshakeable faith in the Lord's eucharistic presence, which is the focus of the invisible presence of all Christian mysteries of faith.'[74]

'Pange Lingua'

St Thomas Aquinas is not only doctor of the Eucharist but mystic and poet of the Eucharist. Tears streamed from his eyes at the altar. When he elevated the Host, he whispered, 'Tu Rex gloriae, Christe, tu Patris sempiternus es Filius', Thou art the King of Glory, O Christ, thou art the everlasting Son of the Father! When Viaticum was brought to him, he crawled from his deathbed and prostrated himself in adoration. Once, having struggled and prayed to resolve a disputed question of Eucharistic doctrine, he was given the grace of a vision of Christ, who gave him this reassurance:

> You have written well concerning this Sacrament of my Body, and you have well and truthfully resolved the problem which has been put to you so far as it is possible to be known on earth and described in words.[75]

In 1264, at the request of Pope Urban IV, St Thomas composed hymns and prayers for the new feast of Corpus Christi. There are no serious grounds for doubting his authorship.[76] The Mass sequence ('Lauda Sion') and the office hymns ('Pange, lingua gloriosi', 'Sacris sollemniis', and 'Verbum supernum prodiens') are triumphs of Latin literature. The beauty of the verse radiates the truth of the doctrine. The Eucharist is a mystery so

---

[74] *Prolegomena*, vol. 1 of *Theodramatik* (Einsiedeln, 1973), 106; ET, *Prolegomena*, vol. 1 of *Theodrama* (San Francisco, 1988), 116.

[75] Kenelm Foster, O.P., ed., *The Life of St Thomas Aquinas: Biographical Documents* (London and Baltimore, 1959), 37.

[76] See J.-P. Torrell, O.P., *Initiation à saint Thomas d'Aquin: Sa personne et son oeuvre* (Paris, 1993), 189–99.

marvellous that the mind of Thomas searches beyond prose for its praise: 'Pange, lingua', 'Of the glorious Body telling, O my tongue, its mysteries sing . . .'

The glorious Body of Christ is in this Sacrament, says St Thomas, in truth, in reality, and not just by figure or sign.[77] He gives three reasons why this bodily presence of God-made-man is 'fitting' (*conveniens est*, *competit*), that is to say, three ways in which it harmonizes beautifully with the other truths of Divine Revelation. First, the Real Presence demonstrates the superiority of the New Law. The sacrifices of the Old Law were a shadow, a figure, preparing for the Truth that was to come. By contrast, the Sacrifice of the New Law contains Christ Himself, who suffered for us; it contains Him not merely by way of sign or figure but really and truly, 'in the truth of the thing', *in rei veritate*. 'Types and shows have their ending, for the newer rite is here. . . .' Secondly, the Real Presence fits in perfectly with Christ's charity, the love that led the Son of God to assume a true body of human nature for our salvation. Now charity is a kind of friendship, and it is the very law of friendship, as Aristotle said, that friends should live together. It was, therefore, a beautiful act of friendship on the part of Our Lord to give us His bodily presence on earth by way of the Sacrament while we wait for His bodily presence in Heaven by way of reward.

> He has not deprived us of His bodily presence in this pilgrimage of ours but joins us to Himself in this Sacrament through the reality (*veritatem*) of His Body and Blood. For this reason He says, 'He who eats my flesh and drinks my blood abides in me, and I in Him' (Jn 6:57). Hence this Sacrament is a sign of supreme charity, and lifts up our hope, because it joins Christ so intimately to us.[78]

[77] Cf. ST 3a 75, 1.
[78] Ibid.

The third reason why the Real Presence is so fitting, such a beautiful gift, is that it perfects man's faith in the unseen. Our faith is in both Christ's divinity and in His humanity, the two natures united hypostatically in the Divine Person of the Word. Now faith has to do with unseen realities, and so just as the one Person of the Son offers us His divinity in an invisible manner, so here, in the Sacrament, He offers His humanity in an invisible way. 'Blessed are they who do not see and yet believe. . . .' The hiddenness of the Real Presence is a mark of His chivalrous Heart: He does not force His beauty upon us, with a fury of obviousness. He invites us into the bridal surrender, to faith in Him in obscurity. This truth is expressed poetically in the hymn 'Adoro te devote', traditionally ascribed to St Thomas[79] and superbly translated by Hopkins:

> On the Cross thy godhead made no sign to men;
> Here thy very manhood steals from human ken;
> Both are my confession, both are my belief,
> And I pray the prayer of the dying thief.[80]

The risen humanity of Christ in all its beauty is substantially present in the Blessed Sacrament, but it is hidden by the lowly

[79] It has often been argued that St Thomas could never have written the 'Adoro te' because of the first two lines of the second stanza: 'Visus, tactus, gustus in te fallitur,/ Sed auditu solo tuto creditur', 'Seeing, touching, tasting are in thee deceived;/ How says trusty hearing? That shall be believed.' P.-M. Gy has argued that 'neither poetic emotion nor devotion could have made Thomas write [these words]' ('L'Office du Corpus Christi et la théologie des accidents eucharistiques', *Revue des sciences philosophiques et theologiques* 66 [1982]: 83). Gy's reasoning is straightforward. St Thomas is adamant that 'in this Sacrament there is no deception. The accidents, which are discerned by the senses, are really and truly there' (ST 3a 75, 5, ad 2), and so he would be unlikely, even by way of poetic enthusiasm, to speak of the senses being deceived. However, Father Torrell, having surveyed the arguments for and against, suggests that, even on doctrinal grounds, we do not have to be too negative about Thomas's authorship of this great hymn (Torrell, *Initiation*, 197).

[80] *The Poetical Works of Gerard Manley Hopkins*, ed. N. H. Mackenzie (Oxford, 1990), 113.

accidents of bread. Even though glorified at the Father's right hand, the body of the Son of God pours out its power in silence and simplicity. The ciborium and the monstrance prolong the humility of the manger and the Cross.

'Nobis Datus, Nobis Natus ex Intacta Virgine'

'Given for us, for us descending,/ Of a Virgin to proceed. . . .' On Maundy Thursday and Corpus Christi, the Church does not forget Christmas Day. The beautiful Body substantially present under the appearance of bread is none other than the true body born of the Virgin Mary, the body in which He was crucified, died, and was buried, the body in which He rose from the tomb. On his deathbed, St Thomas Aquinas made a profession of faith in this mystery:

> I truly believe and most certainly know that this is indeed true God and man, Son of the eternal Father, born of the Virgin Mother, the Lord Jesus Christ. This I sincerely believe and profess.[81]

This is the doctrine preached by Fra Angelico in his altarpiece. Our Lady is showing the friars of San Marco the blessed Fruit of her womb. Her hand gently indicates Our Lord, as if to say: 'The eternal Son who took flesh from me now feeds you with that same flesh at this altar. The almighty Word who came in the littleness of human infancy now gives you His whole self, divinity and humanity, under the lowly form of bread.'

On the altar, as in the manger, we have the gift of God the Father. As St Bonaventure says in a Christmas sermon, probably well known to the Dominicans of the Strict Observance:

> I admire . . . the generosity of the Giver, because to the soul who asked Him He gave not only pennies but a person, not a

---

[81] Foster, *Life* (London, 1959), 55.

servant but a Son, and with Him He gave us all that He was, all that He had, all that He could.[82]

In the Holy Eucharist, God the Father gives us the true Body and Blood of His consubstantial Son, His 'All', under the appearances of bread and wine. 'God so loved the world that He gave us His only Son' (Jn 3:16). Those words are not restricted to the Father's gift on Christmas Day and Good Friday. They are true every day, until the end of the age, in Holy Mass and Holy Communion.

Bethlehem and the Altar are also connected by the Holy Spirit. Just as the Holy Spirit fashioned a body for the Father's Son from the flesh of the Virgin Mary, so now, by His power, bread is transubstantiated into the same Body of the Son. In the words of St Paschasius, the greatest theologian of the Carolingian Renaissance:

> Do not be surprised, O man, nor look for the order of nature. But if you believe that flesh to have been truly created from the Virgin Mary in her womb without seed by the power of the Holy Spirit, so that the Word was made flesh, truly believe also that what is confected at the word of Christ by the Holy Spirit is His Body from the Virgin.[83]

'Gloriosi Corporis Mysterium'

Where there is wholeness, there is beauty. Now, says St Thomas, 'it is absolutely necessary according to Catholic faith to confess that the whole Christ is in this Sacrament.'[84] To explain how this is so, he makes a distinction that is fundamental to his theology of the Eucharist. There are two ways in which something of Christ can be present in the Sacrament: *in virtue of the Sacrament*

---

[82] *Sermo 1 in Vigilia Nativitatis Domini*; *Sancti Bonaventurae opera omnia*, vol. 9 (Quaracchi, 1901), 89.

[83] *Liber de Corpore et Sanguine Christi* 4, 3; PL 120, 1279C.

[84] ST 3a 76, 1.

(*ex vi Sacramenti*) and *in virtue of natural concomitance* (*ex naturali concomitantia*). In virtue of the Sacrament, whatever the words uttered say is present *is* present; in virtue of natural concomitance, whatever naturally accompanies the thing that is present is also present. In virtue of the Sacrament, the Body of Christ is present under the appearance of bread and the Blood of Christ is present under the appearance of wine; the whole substance of bread is converted into the whole substance of Christ's Body, the whole substance of wine converted into the whole substance of Christ's Blood. However, in virtue of natural concomitance, the Blood is present with the Body under the appearance of bread, and the Body is present with the Blood under the appearance of wine.[85] Moreover, under each appearance, the soul of Jesus and His divinity also accompany the Body and Blood.[86] In support, St Thomas quotes St Cyril of Alexandria's *Third Letter to Nestorius*:

> We partake of the Body and the Blood of Christ. It is not ordinary flesh nor even the flesh of someone who is very holy and joined to the Word, sharing His dignity; but it is actually life-giving; it is the very flesh of the Word Himself.[87]

The Hypostatic Union never comes to an end: what God took from the Virgin, He kept. The two natures—the divine and the human—are *inseparably* united in the Word. And so, in virtue of natural concomitance, in virtue of the Hypostatic Union, in having the Body and Blood we have also the divinity of Christ. That is why the Church gives the Blessed Sacrament the adoration due to God alone, expressed, in the Latin Church, by a genuflection. And here, too, is the source of the divinizing effect

---

[85] Ibid., 76, 2.

[86] Ibid., 76, 1, ad 1.

[87] Ibid., 76, 1. St Cyril says that Christ wants us to be united with Him not only spiritually, by faith and charity, but also corporeally. There is to be a union of the human person in his flesh and blood with the Divine Person of the Son in His flesh and blood (cf. *In Joannis Evangelium*, lib. 10; PG 74, 341AB).

of the Eucharist. By feeding men with His Body and Blood, the Son draws them more deeply into His divine life, the life He lives with the Father in the unity of the Holy Spirit. The hidden beauty of the Eucharist is the beauty of the Holy Trinity.

Through the Hypostatic Union, the whole humanity is inseparably united to the divinity in the person of the Son. Through the Resurrection, the Body is inseparably united to the Blood and the Soul. And so through natural concomitance, the whole glorious Christ, the God-Man with all the accidents of His risen radiance, is present in the Eucharist. This is the radiance that Fra Angelico tries to mirror in his paintings.

'Verbum Caro, Panem Verum . . .'

'Word made flesh, by word He maketh/ Very bread His flesh to be.' St Thomas teaches that the Body of Christ does not come to be present in the Eucharist by local movement. The words of consecration do not displace the risen body from Heaven, nor do they deposit it in many different places. No, says Thomas, there is no other way in which the Body of Christ can become present in the Eucharist than by the conversion of the substance of bread into it.[88] This change, Transubstantiation, affects the bread, not the Body of Christ. The consecration brings about a new relationship ('quaedam habitudo')[89] between the impassible Body of Christ in Heaven and the appearance of bread whose substance is converted into the substance of that Body. The transubstantiating Holy Spirit abolishes all distance between ourselves and the glorious flesh of the Father's Son in Heaven. The accidents of bread are the lightest of veils behind which is really and truly the risen Lord in all His heavenly beauty, the incarnate Son shining with the Holy Spirit in the glory of the

[88] Ibid.
[89] Ibid., 76, 6.

Father, the Lamb standing as though slain, adored by the Mother of God and all the angels and saints. In the Mass, Heaven comes down to earth, or rather earth is taken up and given access to Heaven, to the glorified Jesus, who is Heaven's heart, the crown of all the saints.

According to Dr William Hood, it was this faith in the presence of all Heaven with the Eucharistic Jesus that inspired Fra Angelico and the other painters of Dominican altarpieces.

> The Preachers liked . . . to remind themselves that the presence of Christ on their altars . . . literalized the meaning of their office as a simultaneous parallel to the worship of the company of Heaven. To be sure, their worship was carried out in time and space, but it was integrally connected with the invisible beatitude of Paradise by virtue of its taking place in the full presence of the King of Heaven. The altarpieces of all Dominican choirs, not just those by Fra Angelico, thus need to be understood as parts of this liturgical action centred, even for non-Eucharistic worship, on Christ's presence in the Sacrament.[90]

'Et Antiquum Documentum'

'Types and shadows have their ending, for the newer rite is here. . . .' The chief 'type and shadow' of the Eucharist, says St Thomas, is the sacrificed Passover Lamb.[91] This typology indicates that the Mass is a true and proper Sacrifice. Christ is the Lamb of God who takes away the sins of the world, the slaughtered Lamb whose poured-out blood delivers the New Israel from the Egypt of sin and sets their feet on the promised land of the Father. He is present in the Holy Eucharist, and so is His Sacrifice. The Mass is a sacrifice, says St Thomas, because in it the Sacrifice Christ offered on the Cross is 're-presented' (*reprae-*

---

[90] William Hood, *Fra Angelico at San Marco* (London, 1993), 46f.
[91] Cf. ST 3a 73, 6.

sentatur), made really present and offered by the Church through her priests for the living and the dead.[92]

The Sacrifice of the Cross and the Sacrifice of the Mass are one and the same Sacrifice.[93] The Victim offered is the same, and the Priest who offers is the same; only the manner of offering is different. The divine Victim-Priest who on the altar of the Cross offered Himself to the Father in a bloody way now offers Himself to the Father, through priests, in an unbloody way.[94] This is suggested by Fra Angelico by the imposition of a miniature of the Crucifixion at the foot of his altarpiece. On this altar, he is telling us, in this Sacrament, Christ is daily immolated: the Passion of Christ is here re-presented and its fruits poured out.[95] The Church is, as it were, at the foot of the Cross with the Blessed Virgin and St John.[96] The pure sacrifice of the Father's Lamb is not locked away in the closet of history as a mere mental memory but is earthed by the Holy Spirit in the here and now, and thus all its saving power, all its beautifying efficacy, flows forth afresh upon the world. We offer Christ in Eucharistic

---

[92] 'This Sacrament is not only a sacrament but also a sacrifice. Inasmuch as in this Sacrament Christ's Passion is re-presented, the Passion in which Christ "offered Himself as a sacrifice to God" (Eph 5:2), it has the nature of a sacrifice' (ST 3a 79, 7). In similar terms, the Council of Trent speaks of the Mass as a visible sacrifice 'by which the bloody Sacrifice which He was once for all to accomplish on the Cross [is] re-presented' (Council of Trent, twenty-second session, *Doctrine on the Most Holy Sacrifice of the Mass* (1562), chap. 1; DS 1740). The new *Catechism* likewise teaches: 'The Eucharist is thus a sacrifice because it *re-presents* (makes present) the sacrifice of the cross, because it is its *memorial*, and because it *applies* its fruit' (CCC 1366).

[93] 'The Sacrifice offered daily in the Church is not a different sacrifice from the one Christ Himself offered [in His Passion]' (ST 3a 22, 3, ad 2).

[94] 'In the divine Sacrifice which is accomplished in the Mass, the same Christ who offered Himself "once in a bloody way" (cf. Heb 9:14, 27) on the altar of the Cross is contained and offered in an unbloody way' (Council of Trent, twenty-second session, *Doctrine on the Most Holy Sacrifice of the Mass* [1562], chap.2; DS 1743).

[95] '. . . [Q]uotidie immolatur Christus in Sacramento' (cf. ST 3a 83, 1).

[96] 'In the Eucharist the Church is as it were at the foot of the cross with Mary, united with the offering and intercession of Christ' (CCC 1370).

Sacrifice and receive Him in Eucharistic Communion for the glorification of the Trinity and the beautification of our souls and bodies.

There is another importantly aesthetic aspect of St Thomas's theology of the Sacrifice of the Mass and the priesthood. As we have already mentioned, he takes up the Byzantine theology of the priest as the 'icon' of Christ when he says that, in uttering the words of consecration, the priest 'bears the image of Christ' and acts in His 'person and power'.[97] The celebrant of Holy Mass lends Our Lord his voice and gestures; he is the living instrument through which Christ in the Holy Spirit changes bread and wine into His Body and Blood and so renews the Sacrifice of Himself to the Father. Thus not only is the Victim the same both on the Cross and in the Mass, so is the priest—not in reality, says St Thomas, but by way of image and representation.[98]

'O Sacrum Convivium'

The Eucharist, says St Thomas, incorporates us more perfectly into Christ and His Church, preserves and increases the life of His grace in our souls, and gives us a pledge of future glory in both soul and body. In the Sacrament, the whole Christ makes us partake of His integrity, His divine and human *integritas*, and thus of His beauty. When received worthily in Holy Communion, Our Lord makes us one body (incorporate, concorporate) with Himself, and all His fulness as God and man overflows to us.[99] Before Holy Communion, St Thomas prays:

[97] Cf. ST 3a 83, 1, ad 3. See the conclusion to chap. 1, 69 above.

[98] *4 Sent.*, d. 8, q. 2, a. 1, sol. 4.

[99] If Baptism is the beginning of our incorporation into Christ, the Eucharist is its completion (cf. *4 Sent.*, d. 4, q. 2, a. 2, sol. 5, ad 2). Since in the Eucharist there is a 'perfect influence from the Head in the member', incorporation is an effect of the Eucharist (cf. *4 Sent.*, d. 4, q. 2, a. 2e, ad 2). St Cyril of

Most gentle God, grant me so to receive the Body of thy only begotten Son, Our Lord Jesus Christ, which He took from the Virgin Mary, that I may be found worthy to be incorporated into His Mystical Body and to be counted among His members.[100]

The grace of the Head pours out from His soul to ours ('Soul of Christ, sanctify me . . .'), and the glory of His resurrected flesh ('Body of Christ, save me . . .') is placed in our frailty like seed in stubble. Through His given-up Body and poured-out Blood, the eternal Son binds us more closely to His Divine Person, makes us share more radiantly in the divine life He lives with the Father in the unity of the Holy Spirit. 'As the living Father hath sent me, and I live by the Father, so he that eateth me, the same also shall live by me' (Jn 6:58).

Christ through the Blessed Sacrament divinizes us by His grace. 'Just as by coming into the world visibly, He conferred grace on the world . . . so, by coming into man sacramentally, He causes the life of grace.'[101] The Eucharistic Jesus does not just confer Sanctifying Grace and the virtues as dispositions but stirs them into action. If she is in the state of grace and ready to welcome Him, the receiving soul, like a bride, will be made drunk by the sweet goodness of her Groom: 'Eat your fill, lovers; drink, sweethearts, and drink deep' (Knox, Song 5:1). A beautiful act of love for the Lord is the proper effect of eating His Body and drinking His Blood. Moreover, according to St Thomas, even in this life, there is a transfiguration of our bodies through the grace of the Eucharist. 'Although the body is not the immediate subject of grace, the effect of grace overflows from the soul into the body when, in this present life, we yield

---

Jerusalem says that, having partaken of the true Body and Blood of Christ in the Sacrament, a man becomes 'one body and one blood with Christ [*syssômos kai synaimos Christou*]' (*Mystagogia* 4, 3; SC 126B, 136).

[100] *Piae preces*, no. 6.

[101] ST 3a 79, 1.

our members to God as "instruments of justice" (cf. Rom 6:13).'[102] The dear Body of Our Lord calms the storms of concupiscence, washes away the dust of venial sin, and strengthens us to resist temptations to mortal sin. We leave the altar, says Thomas, quoting Chrysostom, 'like lions breathing fire, redoubtable to the devil'.[103]

All this—and Heaven too! The Blessed Sacrament is a pledge of future glory and everlasting happiness. Praying after Holy Communion, St Thomas begs God the Father to welcome the communicant to the feast of unending delight with the Trinity in Heaven: 'I pray thee to deign to bring me, a sinner, to that ineffable banquet, where thou, with thy Son and the Holy Spirit, art to thy saints true light, full satisfaction, everlasting joy, consummate mirth, and perfect happiness.'[104] The Beatific Vision of the Triune God is the consummation of our Eucharistic incorporation into Christ. And the resurrection of our bodies, too, is an effect of our receiving of Our Lord's Body: 'He who eats my flesh and drinks my blood has eternal life; and I will raise him up on the last day' (Jn 6:55). The glorified Body and Blood of the Saviour enter our lowly bodies as the germ of their future resurrection. As St Cyril of Alexandria says, His flesh, united to the Word who is Life, is placed in our flesh as 'the seed of immortality, abolishing all the corruption that is in us'.[105]

Among the Dominican Doctors, it is especially St Albert who develops a theological aesthetic of the Eucharist. According to his interpretation, when the divine Bridegroom feeds the Bride with the sweetness of Himself, He cries out: 'Quam pulchra es, et quam decora, carissima, in deliciis', How beautiful art thou, and how comely, my dearest, in delights! (Song 7:6). The delightful Body of Christ, received in the Eucharist, 'adorns the

---

[102] Ibid., 3a 79, 1, ad 3.
[103] Ibid., 79, 6.
[104] *Piae preces*, no. 8.
[105] *In Joannis Evangelium*, lib. 4, 2 (6:54); PG 73, 581C.

heart of the receiver with chastity and inflames it with charity'.[106] Albert gets the Bride to respond in the person of Esther: 'Valde mirabilis es, Domine, et facies tua plena est gratiarum', Thou, my Lord, art very admirable, and thy face is full of graces (Esther 15:17). Yes, says Albert, in the Blessed Sacrament, the whole Christ is truly contained, with His whole 'face' full of graces: consecrating virginity by His birth, beautifying everyday existence by His life, showing the grace of truth in His words, proving the power of grace in His miracles, showing the efficacy of grace in His death.[107] Even now, says Albert, through the Eucharistic Body of Jesus, we share in the radiance (*claritas*) of Trinitarian life: 'And the radiance which thou hast given me, I have given to them: that they may be one, as we also are one. I in them, and thou in me, that they may be made perfect in one' (Jn 17:22f.).

> The radiance that the Father gave to the Son to make perfect is the radiance by which He shines in all the members of His Mystical Body. In all of them, the radiance of Christ shines and sheds its light. . . . We can have no radiance unless the radiance of the Son of God shines in us. . . . So, then, by pouring Himself into us spiritually and sacramentally, He gives us the radiance that the Father gave Him to perfect in the world, and so we are one with His very Body. . . . Thus, through the divinity, the Father, consubstantial with the Son, shines in Christ the man according to His humanity. And the Son shines in the Father according to one and the same most radiant substance of the divinity. Now if in this way Christ shines in us, we are 'made perfect in one' in the radiance of grace, which is a sign of the eternal radiance of glory. Yes, in glory, we shall shine, through the inpouring into us of the Godhead of the Father and the Son and the Holy Spirit.[108]

[106] *De Eucharistiae Sacramento, pars 6, sermo 24*, no. 2, 1 and 2; *Beati Alberti Magni opera*, ed. A. Borgnet, vol. 13 (Paris, 1891), 766.

[107] Cf. *De Eucharistia*, d. 1, cap. 6; *Beati Alberti Magni opera omnia*, vol. 38 (Paris, 1900), 215.

[108] Ibid., 211f.

How, ask the Church's Fathers and Doctors, can we despair of a final beauty for the whole man when the whole man is fed by the whole beautiful God-Man in the Sacrament? [109]

The Worthiness of the Liturgy

Christ in all His matchless beauty is substantially present in the Eucharist, and His Church strives to worship that beauty with all the accidental beauty of her sacred art—by vestments and vessels, by chant and icons, by the consecrated space of her temples. The Bride knows that no human art can be worthy of her Spouse, who is the eternal Son and Splendour of the Father. Her sense of poverty never leaves her: 'Nigra sum, sed formosa', I am black but comely (Song 1:4). 'Kyrie eleison', she prays, 'Domine non sum dignus.' She knows, as Balthasar points out, that 'it would be ridiculous and blasphemous to want to respond to the glory of God's grace with a counter-glory produced from . . . creaturely resources.' [110] The hidden beauty is always greater than the visible forms.

The destruction of images is the sin of sacrilege, but the discernment of images is common prudence. There is not only good art but *kitsch*. Human malice can twist to an evil end anything good and beautiful, including art. It is possible for men to be so absorbed by the beauty of the image that the person it represents is forgotten; that is beauty's vulnerability. [111] It was to address these dangers that St Bernard (in the twelfth century) wrote his *Apology to Abbot William* and St John of the Cross (in the sixteenth century) the closing chapters of *The Ascent of Mount Carmel*. Monks, says Bernard, do not enter the monastery

---

[109] This is, of course, Our Lord's own teaching in John 6:54. Cf. St Irenaeus, *Adversus haereses* 5, 2, 2–3; PG 7, 1124B–1128B.

[110] Hans Urs von Balthasar, 'The Worthiness of the Liturgy', *New Elucidations* (San Francisco, 1986), 130.

[111] See 35f. above.

for the aesthetic delight of their senses (radiant sights for the eyes or soothing sounds for the ears), but to surrender themselves to Christ.[112] San Juan presents much the same argument. We must be on our guard, he says, against rejoicing more in the ornamentation of an image than in the person represented.[113] The image is meant to stir our wills to devotion to Christ and His saints, not to pamper them with sensible pleasure. We should not allow our senses to be absorbed in the accidents but should raise our spirits to the subject represented.[114] We must prefer nothing—*nada, nada, nada*—to the love of Christ, not even the loveliest image of Christ. Like St Thérèse before the Virgin of the Smile, the man who would venerate the holy icons must gaze with the loving attention of a child, not the peering curiosity of the connoisseur.

Although abuse of images is always possible, the Church does not, cannot, abandon her iconographic mission. The uncontainable God has been sheltered, in the flesh, by the womb and arms of the Virgin. The human face of the eternal Son, lovelier beyond all others, does not elude all imaging, for human eyes have beheld its glory (cf. Jn 1:14; 1 Jn 1:1). The divine Word speaks in human words, sanctifying men's tongues for new poetic praise. He has brought to earth the songs of the halls of Heaven. The sacred art of His Church is, therefore, her delight and dogmatic duty.

> The fine arts are rightly numbered among the noblest expressions of human genius. This is especially true of religious art and its highest achievement, namely, sacred art. By their very nature both are intended to express in some way, by human endeavour,

[112] *Apologia ad Guillelmum Abbatem* 12, 28; *Sancti Bernardi opera*, ed. J. Leclercq and H. Rochais, vol. 3 (Rome, 1963), 104f. See also C. Rudolph, *The Things of Greater Importance: Bernard of Clairvaux's* Apologia *and the Medieval Attitude toward Art* (Philadelphia, 1990), passim.

[113] *The Ascent of Mount Carmel* 3, 35, 2; *The Collected Works of St. John of the Cross* (Washington, D.C., 1991), 331.

[114] Ibid., 3, 37, 2; 336.

the infinite beauty of God. The more single-mindedly they aim
at turning men's minds devoutly towards God, the more they
will be dedicated to God and the increase of His praise and
glory. Holy Mother Church has, therefore, always been the
friend of the fine arts. She has constantly sought out the service
of the arts and trained artists, with this end chiefly in view, that
everything pertaining to divine worship should be worthy,
decorous, and beautiful, signs and symbols of the realities of
Heaven.[115]

Conclusion
Pastoral Theology, Eucharistic Theology

A shepherd herds his sheep, but, as anyone who has a little Latin
knows, a pastor *feeds* them. Pastoral theology must, therefore, be
Eucharistic theology. The pastors of the Church are the icons
and instruments of the *Bonus Pastor* Himself: through them, He
not only leads the flock into the fold but brings it to pasture, to
the banquet of His Body, Blood, Soul, and Divinity. By the gift
of Himself in the Sacrament, the Lamb-Shepherd takes His
sheep to the heights of holiness, into the supreme beauty of the
Trinity. The Eucharist, as St Thomas says, is holy not just in
relation to something else but in itself, for the Eucharist is
Christ, true God made true man, the Author of all Holiness.[116]
Those who devoutly offer themselves in union with Him in the
Sacrifice, those who with reverence receive Him in the Sacrament, are transformed by the Holy Spirit more and more into
His likeness, the likeness of the Father's eternal Son. The saints
in the San Marco altarpiece—the Queen of All Saints and her
servants—are the pledge that the beauty of holiness is not a

---

[115] Second Vatican Council, *Sacrosanctum concilium*, no. 122.
[116] Cf. ST 3a 73, 1, ad 3.

mere dream. From this altar, they say, from this tabernacle, the Splendour of the Father showers His loveliness on the world.

> What you were seeking from afar, Eternity even
>   now accessible to every sense,
> Raise your eyes and hold them fixed before you:
>   It is here.
> Just look at the Azyme in the monstrance.
> This object amid the dry paper flowers is He
>   who is Highest Beauty. . . .
> The veil of things at one point is made
>   transparent for me.
> I embrace at last the substance through the
>   accident! [117]

---

[117] Paul Claudel, 'La Messe la-bas', in *Oeuvre poétique* (Paris, 1967), 509.

III

Tota Pulchra

THE BEAUTY OF OUR LADY AND THE RENEWAL OF CHRISTIAN CULTURE

The great Catholic writer J. R. R. Tolkien once confessed that it was upon Our Blessed Lady that his entire 'perception of beauty, both in majesty and simplicity, [was] founded'.[1] The aesthetic of Fra Angelico was likewise Marian in its foundation. Consider the San Marco altarpiece. Our Lady's beauty is everywhere. Angelico inscribed on her mantle a text from the Little Office of the Blessed Virgin: 'I am the Mother of fairest love and of holy hope.'[2] In the distance can be seen the tranquil ocean, the sure sign of Mary, the guiding star of the sea. The bay is bounded by a forest of palms, cedars, and cypresses, all symbols of the fruitful purity of the Seat of Wisdom: 'I was exalted like a cedar in Libanus, and as a cypress tree on Mount Sion. I was exalted like a palm tree on Cades, and as a rose plant in Jericho. . . . As the vine I have brought forth a pleasant odour, and my flowers are the fruit of honour and riches' (Sir 24:13–17). Angelico has opened a casement onto Paradise, the park that is Mary, in which Jesus, the Tree of Life, is planted by the Father

---

[1] *The Letters of J. R. R. Tolkien*, ed. H. Carpenter (Boston, 1981), 172. Tolkien is here writing to Fr Robert Murray, S.J.

[2] Sir 24:24; William Hood, *Fra Angelico at San Marco* (London, 1993), 108.

through the overshadowing of the Holy Spirit. Here is the 'enclosed garden' (Song 4:12) of inviolate virginity, the 'garden of delights' (Song 4:16), through which blows the South Wind of God, setting the fragrance of His grace astir. As William Hood says in his study of Fra Angelico:

> Like a perfume the imagery of the Virgin thus suffuses the entire altarpiece. And like a perfume its scent is not contained. Rather, as in all Dominican high altarpieces before Fra Angelico's time, the Virgin—as the Mother of God, the Throne of Wisdom, as the faithful protectress of the Order of Preachers, and as the personification of the Church—created the ambience in which the painter made Christ accessible to spiritual sight through the eyes of the flesh.[3]

Here at last is the unspoilt Daughter Sion foreseen by the prophets, the lovely Bride praised by Solomon: 'Tota pulchra es, amica mea', All fair art thou, O my love, and there is no spot in thee (Song 4:7). All the beauty for soul and body that the Son of God brought into the world, all the loveliness He wants to lavish on mankind, is summed up in, and mediated by, the person of His Ever-Virgin Mother, 'a woman clothed with the sun, the moon under her feet, and on her head a crown of twelve stars' (Rev 12:1). If there is beauty, it is here. If there is a theological aesthetic, it is She.[4]

In this chapter, I shall, first of all, try to explain why the Tradition ascribes supreme beauty to the Mother of God. Since beauty is the splendour of the truth, my hope is that this Mariological aesthetic will shed a fresh light on the Church's Mariological dogmas. Secondly, I shall argue that true devotion to the Blessed Virgin is the irreplaceable key to the renewal of Christian culture, to the building up of a civilization of love.

---

[3] Ibid.

[4] As Balthasar says, 'Mary's image radiates with the evidential power which comes from having been created and shaped by the form of revelation' (H 1, 544; GL 1, 565).

The San Marco Altarpiece: *Madonna and Child*. (Detail)

1. "The Fairest Mother That Ever Was Alive"
The Beauty of Our Blessed Lady

Types of Beauty

The Blessed Virgin, said the fifteenth-century poet John Lydgate, is the 'Fairest Mother that ever was alive'.[5] Throughout the Christian centuries, those homely English words were echoed a thousandfold in every tongue, their meaning repeated in every art form. Every poet and painter, all the sculptors and church builders, wanted to praise the Virgin Mother.

In the catacomb of Priscilla, Our Lady appears as the Mother of Jacob's Star. The Byzantines paint her as the enthroned Theotokos and merciful Mediatrix, the way that leads to the God-Man (*Hodêgêtria*), the Virgin of tender kindness (*Eleousa*). Giotto, fired by Francis, gives the world her smile and the laughter of her baby. Botticelli, swayed by Savonarola, suggests the sorrow to come.

When Dante reaches Paradise, he finds the beauty of the Son of God most perfectly mirrored in the Rose-Mary, in whom He flowered in the flesh. The *Vergine Madre* is 'the lovely sapphire/ Whose grace ensapphires the heaven's brightest sphere'.[6] The beauty of Beatrice is but a shaft of her shining.

> I looked above and, as the orient scene
>   At dawn exceeds the beauty of the west,
>   Where the declining sun has lately been,
>
> So, mounting as from vale to mountain-crest,
>   These eyes beheld, at the remotest rim,
>   A radiance surpassing all the rest.[7]

[5] 'The Child Jesus to Mary the Rose', in *I Sing of a Maiden: The Mary Book of Verse*, ed. Sister M. Thérèse (New York, 1947), 114.

[6] *Paradiso* 23, 73f., 101ff.; *Dantis Aligherii Divina Comoedia edita mandatu Pauli VI Pont. Max.* (Vatican, 1965), 602f.; ET, M. Musa (New York, 1995), 529.

[7] *Paradiso* 31, 118–23; 666; ET, Dorothy L. Sayers and Barbara Reynolds (Baltimore, 1962), 330.

Inspired by Dante, Chaucer, too, 'sing[s] to the singer of the Magnificat'[8] and saves for her his sweetest lines:

> O Mother-Maid, Maid-Mother, chaste and free!
> O bush unburnt, burning in Moses' sight,
> Thou that didst ravish down from Deity
> Upon thy humbleness the Spirit's flight
> That lit upon thy heart, and in whose might
> The Word took flesh, help me to tell my story
> In reverence of thee and of thy glory![9]

Chaucer asks Our Lady to help him. His golden words seem like tin when he unwraps them in her presence. St Bonaventure, in a sermon on the Assumption, acknowledges a similar poverty:

> *Carissimi*, dearly beloved, the excellent sublimity of the glorious Virgin so surpasses human capacity that words do not suffice to unfold it. That is why the Holy Spirit, who filled her with the Gifts and the Virtues, speaking through the Prophets and the other Doctors of Sacred Scripture, praises her in many different ways, not only by plain words, but also by figures and metaphors.[10]

Europe's greatest cathedrals were dedicated to her—Paris, Reims, Amiens, Chartres, Laon, Senlis.[11] From at least the thirteenth century, every church of the West will have its own Lady Chapel. In Durham Cathedral, during the Middle Ages, the beauty of the Mother of God pervaded every stone. Her image was high on the Neville Screen. On the feast of the Assumption, the high altar was hung with 'all white damask, set with pearls

---

[8] G. K. Chesterton, *Chaucer* (New York, 1932), 119.

[9] 'The Prioress's Tale', *The Canterbury Tales*, trans. into modern English by Nevill Coghill (Baltimore, 1952), 193.

[10] *De Assumptione B. V. M. sermo 4*; *Sancti Bonaventurae opera omnia*, vol. 9 (Quaracchi, 1901), 695.

[11] See E. Mâle, *Religious Art in France: The Thirteenth Century* (Princeton, 1984), 233ff.

and precious stones'. The Lady Altar, made of blue marble, stood in the Galilee Chapel. Its wainscot was 'devised and furnished with most heavenly pictures so lively in colours and gilding as that they did greatly adorn the said altar'. A daily Votive Mass of Our Lady was sung there by the Master of the Song School and his choristers. On the north side of the Galilee was the altar of Our Lady of Pity 'with her picture carrying Our Saviour on her knee as He was taken from the Cross, a very dolorous aspect'.[12] The bishop may have been Durham's prince, but its Queen was the Mother of God.[13]

The Doctors of the Middle Ages, like the Fathers before them, found beauty in Mary and Mary in beauty. In the *De laudibus Sanctae Mariae*,[14] Richard of St Laurent, thirteenth-century Dean of Rouen, devoted two long chapters to the spiritual and bodily beauty of Our Lady.[15] St Bonaventure quotes St Bernard: the Holy Virgin is *tota pulchra* because 'she is most fair of face, most whole in body, most holy in spirit.'[16] In Heaven, she enjoys the risen splendour of her Son in body as well as soul, but even on earth, the glory of her person as Mother of God and the beauty of her soul as full of grace shone through a face that was fittingly fair. Hers was a beauty, not of glamorous sensuality,

[12] *Rites of Durham: Being a Description or Brief Declaration of All the Ancient Monuments, Rites and Customs Belonging or Being within the Monastical Church of Durham before the Suppression*, Surtees Society, no. 107 (1903), 43f.

[13] From the earliest times, the bishop enjoyed temporal as well as spiritual powers and ranked as a Count Palatine. As the old tag has it, 'quicquid rex habet extra episcopus habet intra.'

[14] This was long attributed to St Albert and well known by Angelico and Antoninus.

[15] ' "All fair art thou", that is, in body and in soul: in body, through the integrity of incorruption and the unimpaired purity of all the senses; in the soul, not only all fair through humility, but very beautiful, most beautiful, through the perfect plenitude of all the virtues' (*De laudibus Sanctae Mariae; Beati Alberti Magni opera omnia*, ed. A. Borgnet, vol. 36 [Paris, 1898], 274).

[16] *De Annuntiatione B. V. M. sermo* 5, no. 1; *Sancti Bonaventurae opera omnia* 9:679.

but of innocent simplicity. The world's first love and loveliest woman was the Immaculate Conception.

When the medievals read the two books of Scripture and nature, they discovered types of Our Lady's loveliness on every page and chapter, in every tree and flower. Her divine motherhood was promised in all shrines of the divine presence: in Ark and Tent and Temple.[17] Her virginity was prefigured in the ancient miracles of sudden fruitfulness and unsullied freshness: the Burning Bush, Aaron's Flowering Rod, Gideon's Moist Fleece, the Closed Gate, the Stone Cut without Hands.[18] The fair faces of salvation history are but a faint shadow of the immaculate loveliness to come: Eve, of course, but also Rebecca, Rachel, Judith, Esther, the Bride of the Canticle, the Valiant Woman of Proverbs.[19] The Virgin of Nazareth is the fairest flower of the Jewish race, Israel immaculate, the purest seed of Abraham. It is

[17] See, among countless examples, St Bonaventure's sermon on the text, '*Visa est arca testamenti Dei in templo eius*', 'The ark of His testament was seen in His temple' (Rev 11:19) (*In Nativitate B.V.M. sermo* 5; *Sancti Bonaventurae opera omnia* 9:715).

[18] St Bernard weaves most of these images into a single paragraph in his second homily 'In Praise of the Virgin Mother': 'What was shown to Moses in the Bush and the Fire (cf. Ex 3:2), to Aaron in the Rod and the Flower (cf. Nb 17:8), to Gideon in the Fleece and the Dew (cf. Jg 6:36ff.): the same was clearly foreseen by Solomon in the Valiant Woman and her price (cf. Prov 31:10), was proclaimed still more clearly by Jeremiah in the Woman and the Man she was to encompass (cf. Jer 31:22), was declared with most clarity of all by Isaiah, who spoke of God and the Virgin (cf. Is 7:14), and finally was exposed to view when Gabriel greeted Mary' (*In laudibus Virginis Matris* 2, 12; *Sancti Bernardi opera*, ed. J. Leclercq and H. Rochais, vol. 4 [Rome, 1966], 28f.). These images appear also in liturgical poetry and in the glass and sculpture of the great cathedrals (see F. J. E. Raby, *A History of Christian-Latin Poetry: From the Beginnings to the Close of the Middle Ages* [Oxford, 1927], 363ff., and Mâle, *Religious Art in France*, 152ff.).

[19] St Bonaventure looks for foreshadowings of Mary's beauty among all the holy women of the Old Covenant: for example, he says that Abraham symbolizes God he Father, Isaac typifies Christ, and Rebecca, the Virgin Mary (cf. *De Annuntiatione B.V.M. sermo* 2, no. 1; 660). Esther is a figure of the Blessed Virgin both in name and in reality (cf. *De Assumptione B.V.M. sermo* 4; 695).

through the flesh He takes from her that the Son of God becomes Son of David, Son of Abraham, a Jew.[20] All the graces
given to the Patriarchs were a preparation for the fulness of grace
bestowed on the Mother of the Messiah. The Byzantine liturgy
acclaims the Daughter of Sion on behalf of the whole Tradition
in West and East: 'The whole choir of the Prophets, instructed
by God, proclaimed the mystery of thy divine and ineffable conceiving of the Word of God, who was born of thee, O Virgin
mother, for thou didst reveal true and ancient decree.'[21]

When they closed their Bibles and gazed at the sky or walked
through the fields, the Fathers and Medievals found a thousand
reminders of Mary: 'Lady's mantle', 'Lady's glove', 'Lady-
smock', 'Marigold'. In a fourteenth-century *Plantaire*, a French
Dominican lists the healing properties of common herbs and

[20] From at least the time of St Irenaeus, most of the Fathers and Doctors of
the Church have taught that Our Lady, like St Joseph, was of the house and
lineage of David (cf. St Irenaeus, 'ex fructu ventris David, hoc est ex David
Virgine', *Adversus haereses* 3, 9, 2; PG 7, 870B). St John Damascene says that
Mary is 'of the root of Jesse, the tribe of Judah, the family of David, and the
seed of Abraham' (*Expositio fidei*; PG 95, 426C). St Thomas tells us that, according to Jewish custom, a woman has to marry a husband who belongs to
the same tribe as her father (cf. Nb 36:6f.; St Thomas, *Lectura super Matthaeum*,
cap. 1). If this is true, and it is, then the hideous sin of anti-Semitism is a sin
against the beauty of Mary. As Léon Bloy said at the time of the Dreyfus case
'anti-Semitism . . . is the most horrible blow yet suffered in [the] ever-
continuing Passion [of Our Lord]: it is the bloodiest and the most unforgivable
because He receives it upon His Mother's face, and at the hands of Christians'
(*Pilgrim of the Absolute* [New York, 1947], 268). This truth was not forgotten
during the Middle Ages. In his *Explanatio Sacri Epithalamii in Matrem Sponsi*,
the English Augustinian William of Newburgh († c. 1199) describes Our
Lady's intercessions for her own beloved race: 'We should know that the merits of the merciful Mother greatly help the salvation of the people of Israel.
How insistently, do you think, does she daily pray to her almighty Son for her
race? . . . Remember, Son, she says, that you have taken your flesh from them,
and in and by that flesh you worked salvation on earth. They must therefore
share in your spiritual goods, of whose flesh you were not ashamed' (*Explanatio* 3, 5; ed. J. C. Gorman [Fribourg, 1960], 152; cited in H. Graef, *Mary: A
History of Doctrine and Devotion*, vol. 1 [London, 1963], 259).

[21] J. Ledit, *Marie dans la liturgie de Byzance* (Paris, 1976), 64.

plants and then shows how all these qualities are to be found, in a spiritual sense, in Our Lady. For example, fennel and mandrake symbolize her courtesy, while balsam and laurel evoke her mercy.[22] The men of the Middle Ages read the book of nature as they read the Bible—as a tract of senses, a sacramental system, a book of signs written by the divine Poet Himself.[23] Since all things were created through the eternal Word and speak to us of Him, it seemed only natural that all things should speak also of the Mother of the Word.

St John Damascene, poet-theologian of the Christian East, speaks for the Fathers who precede him and the Doctors who follow him, including Angelico: the Theotokos is 'the beautification of the human race, the ornament of all creation, through whom all creation is blessed'.[24]

The Glories of Mary for the Sake of her Son:
The Beauty of the Divine Motherhood

'We praise the glories of Mary', said Cardinal Newman, 'for the sake of her Son.'[25] There is nothing self-admiring about the beauty of Our Lady. She is the Mother of Fairest Love, a self-humbling love, innocent of all narcissism. It is for Christ and to the glory of the Father, by the grace of the Holy Spirit, that Our Lady is 'all fair'. God the Father makes her beautiful in the Holy

---

[22] *A 'Plantaire' in Honour of the Blessed Virgin: Taken from a French Manuscript of the Fourteenth Century*, ed. Sister M. A. Savoic (Washington, D.C., 1933), passim.

[23] 'In the world, everything is symbol. The sun, the constellations, the light, the night, the seasons, all speak a solemn language. What did medieval man think about in winter, when the days grew short and the night seemed determined to triumph forever over light? He thought of the long centuries of half-light before Christ's coming, and understood that light and darkness also have their role in the divine comedy' (Mâle, *Religious Art in France*, 35).

[24] *Homilia 1 in Dormitionem B. V. M.* 3; SC 80, 84.

[25] 'The Glories of Mary for the Sake of her Son', *Discourses Addressed to Mixed Congregations*, new ed. (London, 1892), 342ff.

Spirit, even from her conception, because she is to be the Mother of the radiant Son. St Cyril of Alexandria calls Our Lady *kallitokos* as well as *theotokos*, 'bearer of Him who is true beauty' as well as 'bearer of Him who is true God'.[26] Through the Word uncreated, all things were made in their original beauty, and through the Word incarnate, the fairest of the sons of men, all things are to be brought back to beauty. 'Beauty will save the world', said Dostoevsky's Prince Myshkin—a true proposition, but only when by 'beauty' we mean the beauty of the crucified and risen Christ, who gives splendour to our souls in justification and to our bodies in resurrection. And this is no vague dream, some idle wish. It is already a reality in the Theotokos, all-fair by grace from her Conception, all-fair in glory from her Assumption.

Full of Grace

Grace, as the poet says, is 'God's better beauty',[27] the splendour of the soul. From the beginning of her existence, Mary is radiant with a fulness of spiritual beauty in proportion to her dignity as Mother of God. 'O pure Theotokos', sings the Byzantine Church on the feast of the Entry of the Mother of God into the Temple, 'thou hast a clean and shining beauty of soul, and art filled from Heaven with the grace of God.'[28]

Grace conforms the soul into the likeness of Christ.[29] So it is with Mary. Her plenitude of grace gives her by anticipation a likeness to the Son who will take His flesh from her. Hers is a reflected beauty. The woman poet catches the play of light:

---

[26] 'Mother of Beauty, Mother of Greatness, Mother of Light, Mother of Hope' (*De recta fide ad reginas*; PG 76, 1213C).

[27] 'To What Serves Mortal Beauty', in *The Poetical Works of Gerard Manley Hopkins*, ed. N. H. Mackenzie (Oxford, 1990), 183.

[28] *The Festal Menaion* (London, 1969), 190.

[29] See 60ff. above.

'Christ's mirror she of grace and love'.[30] In face and in grace, Mary is like Jesus. When Dante reaches Paradise, St Bernard tells him that contemplating the countenance of the Mother is the best way of preparing to see the glorious face of the Son:

> Now to that face which most resembles Christ
>   lift up thy face; its radiance alone
>   can grant to thee the power to look on Christ.[31]

Five hundred years earlier, the icon-defending Father St Theodore the Studite wrote some poems on the same theme. In one of these, the Mother of God speaks from her icon and sweetly explains that her Son in His humanity is her living image:

> In this picture I carry in my arms the baby who's
>   the image of His Mother,
> my image, Christ the Lord of all,
> the incandescent light of immortality,
> the liberator of the world from the error of the
>   demons.[32]

This expresses a great dogmatic truth. Since Our Lord is conceived by the Holy Spirit without seed, there is only one human person whom He resembles in His humanity, and that is His Virgin Mother.

> In a motherly way I carry the Son depicted
> To show He is a real child of a mother,
> He who in His likeness to the Father is beyond all
>   describing,
> Since He is inseparably twofold in nature.[33]

---

[30] 'Feast of the Annunciation', in *The Complete Poems of Christina Rossetti*, new ed., vol. 2 (London, 1986), 238.

[31] *Paradiso* 32, 85–87; 672; ET, Sayers and Reynolds, 336.

[32] P. Speck, ed., *Theodorus Studites: Jamben auf verschiedene Gegenstände* (Berlin, 1968), 185.

[33] Ibid., 187.

The Son who is the Image of the Father in His divinity is the image of the Mother in His humanity. What is more, He who is the uncreated Image of the divine Father becomes the image of the human Mother precisely in order to restore the created image of God in man to its original beauty. As the Byzantine liturgy sings on the Sunday of Orthodoxy:

> The uncircumscribed Word of the Father became circumscribed, taking flesh from thee, O Theotokos, and He has restored the sullied image to its ancient glory, filling it with the divine beauty.[34]

In the immaculate Virgin, the divine image in man shines forth with unblemished beauty. Like Mother, like Son.

Immaculate Conception

According to the teaching of the Catholic Church, the Blessed Virgin Mary, for the sake of her Son and by His grace, is wholly fair and thus wholly free from the deformity of sin, both Original Sin and actual sin, both venial and mortal sin. In the fourth century, the Syriac 'Harp of the Spirit', St Ephraem, sings to Christ: 'Thou and thy Mother are the only ones who are totally beautiful in every respect; for in thee, O Lord, there is no spot, and in thy Mother no stain.'[35] Later, in the early fifth century, St Augustine says that every man must confess himself a sinner 'except the Blessed Virgin Mary, whom I desire, for the sake of the honour of the Lord, to leave entirely out of the question when the talk is of sin'.[36]

'Tota pulchra es, Maria, et macula originalis non est in te.' All fair art thou, O Mary, and the original stain is not in thee. The

---

[34] Kontakion for the Sunday of Orthodoxy, *The Lenten Triodion* (London, 1978), 306.

[35] *Carmina Nisibena* 27, 8; *Enchiridion Marianum Biblicum et Patristicum*, ed. D. Casagrande (Rome, 1974), 268.

[36] *De natura et gratia* 36, 42; PL 44, 267.

Blessed Virgin is never anything but all fair. Her soul has a spotless radiance from conception. The original stain never defiles her. This loveliness of the Immaculate Conception is a Christ-centred mystery. Its final cause, its purpose, is her mothering of God-made-man: she is immaculately conceived in order to prepare her to be Theotokos. And its meritorious cause is Christ's Sacrifice on Calvary: it is by the power of the Cross, by the Blood of the Lamb, that she is preserved from the stain of Original Sin.

The Immaculate Conception reveals the cosmic proportions of the beautifying work of Christ. From the Cross, the incarnate Art of the Father fills all history with His radiance ('Fulget Crucis mysterium'), adorning even the beginning of His Mother's existence. Thus, as Blessed Duns Scotus saw, Our Lady's Immaculate Conception *is* her redemption. Hers is a preservative redemption, a preredemption. The other sons and daughters of Adam contract the guilt of Original Sin through their descent from him and are then delivered from it through the grace of Jesus Christ. Mary, the New Eve, is preserved by Christ's grace from ever contracting the original stain. 'It is a more excellent benefit', says Scotus, 'to preserve someone from evil than to permit them to fall into evil and afterwards to deliver them from it.'[37] Our Lady is more, not less, indebted to her Redeemer Son than we are.[38]

In his thinking about the sanctification of Our Lady, St Thomas Aquinas wanted to safeguard the truth that the Lord Jesus is the redeemer of all men without exception (cf. Rom 3:23; 5:12, 19). Since Our Lady is redeemed, it followed, in his opinion,

---

[37] *3 Sent.*, d. 3, q. 1, a. 7; *Joannis Duns Scoti opera omnia*, vol. 14 (Paris, 1894), 162.

[38] 'Redeemed in a more exalted fashion, by reason of the merits of her Son and united to Him by a close and indissoluble tie, she is endowed with the high office and dignity of the Mother of the Son of God, and therefore she is also the beloved Daughter of the Father and Temple of the Holy Spirit' (*Lumen Gentium*, no. 53).

that she must first have inherited Original Sin before being set free from it by the grace of her Son.[39] Although attempts continue to be made to present St Thomas as an 'immaculist', Thomists should be content to admit that, in this matter, Scotus the Subtle Doctor grasped what Aquinas the Angelic Doctor failed to see: redemption in Our Lady is a preservation rather than a liberation. As for the Dominicans of the Strict Observance in Angelico's day, though Blessed John Dominic seems to have written a treatise favourable to the doctrine,[40] St Antoninus sticks to St Thomas's position as expressed in the *Summa Theologiae*: Our Lady's sanctification was a liberation from Original Sin through the bestowal of Sanctifying Grace. She was sanctified in the womb, but 'more swiftly' than Jeremiah and the Baptist, perhaps on the same day and hour as the infusion of her rational soul.[41] This opinion continued to be defended by the Thomists, but its days were numbered.[42] Just as Angelico began work on his altarpiece, the Council of Basel solemnly defined the Immaculate Conception. The council was by this time schismatical, and so the decree had no validity; however, it was a milestone on the road to the definition of 1854. The beauty of the Immaculate Conception was winning hearts and minds.

[39] Cf. ST 3a 27, 2.

[40] *De Conceptione Beatissimae Genetricis Dei Mariae* (1390). This work has still not been edited. See R.-O. Oechslin, 'B. Jean Dominici', *Dictionnaire de spiritualité* 8:475.

[41] *Summae sacrae theologiae, iuris pontificii et caesarei pars quarta* (Venice, 1571), 291.

[42] However, in 1475, Vincent Bandelli, a Dominican from Lombardy, published a fiercely polemical work in opposition to the Immaculate Conception (*Libellus recollectorius auctoritatum de veritate Conceptionis B. V. Mariae*). This unhappy document provoked an equally vehement response from many of the defenders of the doctrine. Pope Sixtus IV convoked and presided over a debate between the two sides, including Bandelli. Shortly afterwards, he approved an office of the Conception for the Roman Breviary and Missal, and, in his *Grave nimis* (September 4, 1483), he reprimanded those who condemned the 'immaculists' as heretics. Bandelli never again wrote or spoke on the subject.

Ever-Virgin, Ever-Fair

According to the Fathers and the great medieval Doctors, Our Lady is beautiful in her virginity. In the icons of Byzantium, as in the San Marco altarpiece, the Madonna's veil signifies her virginity, and the veil's three stars its threefold glory: she is virgin before, during, and for ever after giving human birth to the Son of God. 'Come, ye wise', sings St Ephraem the Syrian, 'let us admire the Virgin Mother, David's most lovely daughter, who gave birth to Wonder.'[43] And St John Damascene says that in her 'virginal beauty' the Theotokos is 'more resplendent than the sun'.[44]

The Mother-Maid is beautiful in her conceiving of Christ by the Holy Spirit and without seed. St Thomas Aquinas gives four reasons why it is fitting (*conveniens*) for Christ to be conceived of a Virgin. By 'fitting' he means 'beautiful'. *Convenientia* is a synonym of *consonantia* and *harmonia*. When St Thomas says that anything is 'fitting', he is inviting us to hear the sweet harmonies of the symphony of Divine Revelation, the concord of the Trinity's works in creating and redeeming man. Of St Thomas's four reasons, I should like to consider the first and third. The first reason for the beauty of the Virginal Conception is theocentric: Christ is conceived of a Virgin 'to guard the dignity of the Father who sent Him'.

> Since Christ is the true and natural Son of God, it was not fitting for Him to have a father other than God, lest the dignity of God be transferred to another.[45]

Through conceiving by the Holy Spirit, the Virgin Mary glorifies the Father and the Son: she makes them clearly known, exhibits the radiance of their distinct Persons, saving the dignity of

---

[43] *Enchiridion Marianum*, 250.
[44] *Homilia in Dormitionem B. V. M.* 3, 4; SC 80, 188.
[45] ST 3a 28, 1.

the sending Father and manifesting the identity of the sent Son. There is a beautiful correspondence between the Son's divine generation and His human conception: He who is begotten eternally in His divinity by the Father without a mother is conceived in time in His humanity by the Mother without a father. The flowers of the field, says St Albert, have their father in the heavens (the sun) and their mother on earth (the soil); so it is with the Flower of Flowers that is Christ: sent by the heavenly Father, the Son takes His flesh from the virgin earth of Mary.[46] 'Just as he comes forth from the Father full of the splendours of the saints, so He comes forth from the Mother full of grace and truth.'[47]

The third reason relates to the human nature assumed by the Son of God. The Virginal Conception was in beautiful harmony with 'the dignity of Christ's humanity, in which there was no room for sin'.[48] The sinless Son, the spotless Lamb, has come to take away the sin of the world, to shoulder it as a burden and so destroy it as a barrier. He could not, therefore, come into the world by the means through which Adam's fallen sons contract his sin. He is the New Adam. He comes to make all things new, to regenerate mankind, to give the cosmos a second and immortal spring. It was not fitting, therefore, for Him to enter the world in the stale old way. He is the rejuvenator of the old, and so, as Pope St Leo the Great says, there is a vernal newness about the manner of His conception and birth: He comes into this lowly world 'in a new order, by a new birth'.[49]

The Son of God is not only conceived in the pure Virgin without seed, He is also born of her without corruption. Christ

[46] *Enarrationes in primam partem Evangelii Lucae; Beati Alberti Magni opera omnia*, ed. A. Borgnet, vol. 22 (Paris, 1894), 52.

[47] Ibid., 196.

[48] ST 3a 28, 1.

[49] Cf. DS 294.

is beauty, and His style, the way He acts in His human nature,[50] is beautiful. His very entry into this world is by a beautiful path. His conception is virginal, and so is His birth. At the beginning of His earthly life as at the end, He preserves integrity, that wholeness which is the hallmark of beauty: He comes forth from an 'intact Virgin' just as He rises from an 'intact tomb'.[51] Incarnation is not invasion. In becoming man, the Son of God neither abandons His divinity nor absorbs our humanity. The uniting of man's nature to God's in the person of the Word is an act of infinite gentleness; it takes place 'without separation or division, without confusion or change'. He comes to beautify, not destroy, to raise up, not to crush.[52] In taking flesh from the pure Virgin, He does not employ her as a passive instrument but, by a divine courtesy, asks for and makes possible her active consent. And as He enters Mary's womb, so He leaves it—in a beautiful way, without hurt or harm of its maidenly wholeness. In the words of St Bonaventure, God the Son is born of the Virgin in His human nature, like a flower from a branch, 'not by corrupting the branch but by making it better, not by opening it, but by beautifying it'.[53] The Divine Person of the eternal Son can do what no human person can do: He chooses not only the woman who gives Him human birth but also the manner of His birth. He wants it to be, as He Himself is, a gift of pure joy.[54] St

[50] What St Maximus calls the *tropos* of His operations (cf. *Opuscula theologica et polemica* 10; PG 91, 137A).

[51] Cf. St Peter Chrysologus, *Sermo 75*, 3; CCSL 24A, 460.

[52] As St Thomas says, quoting St Augustine, the Son of God comes to heal corruption, not to inflict it (cf. ST 3a 28, 2).

[53] *Vigilia Nativitatis Domini sermo 12*, no. 1; *Sancti Bonaventurae opera omnia* 9:100.

[54] As St Gregory of Nyssa says, 'His existence [as man] did not begin in pleasure, nor did He come forth through pain. . . . Since woman brought death to human nature through sin, she was condemned to give birth in pain and labour (cf. Gen 3:16). It was necessary that the Mother of Life should conceive her child with joy and perfect the act of giving birth in joy' (*In Canticum Canticorum, homilia* 13; PG 44, 1053B).

Antoninus takes up an idea of Damascene's: the pains Our Lady was spared in Bethlehem she endured on Calvary; the birth of the Head was in joy, but the birth of the Mystical Body was in sorrow.[55]

Our Lady is virgin not only before and during the birth of Jesus but also for ever after. She is 'Ever-Virgin' (*semper virgo, aeiparthenos*). St Thomas shows how the heresy of Helvidius, who taught that Mary bore other children after Jesus, dishonours both the Three Divine Persons and the two human persons of Mary and Joseph. First, it disparages the perfection of Christ (and therefore the Father). Since Christ is the only-begotten of the divine Father, it is fitting, beautifully right, that He should be the only-begotten of the human Mother. Secondly, the denial of Our Lady's perpetual virginity offends the Holy Spirit, for the virginal womb was His shrine. Thirdly, the heresy dishonours the holiness of the Mother of God: it makes her seem ungrateful, as if she were not content with such a great Son. Finally, Helvidius insults St Joseph: he accuses him of extreme presumption, attempting to violate the one who, as he knew by the angel's revelation, had conceived by the Holy Spirit.[56]

'And he knew her not till she brought forth her firstborn Son' (Mt 1:25). Leaning on the Fathers, St Thomas shows how this text does not impugn the perpetual virginity of Our Lady; on the contrary, it reveals her maidenly beauty. The simplest explanation of it comes from St Jerome. The 'till' refers to an indefinite period of time. It does not mean that there was a carnal 'knowing' after the birth of Christ. Jerome and Thomas give another example of this usage: when David says, 'Our eyes are unto the Lord our God till He have pity on us' (Ps 22:2), he does not mean that, once we have obtained God's pity, our eyes will turn away from God. St Thomas also mentions two other

---

[55] Cf. St John Damascene, *De fide orthodoxa* 4, 14; PG 94, 1161CD; St Antoninus, *Summae sacrae theologiae*, 379ff.

[56] Cf. ST 3a 28, 3.

Patristic interpretations. First, there is St John Chrysostom, who says that, before she gave birth, St Joseph did not know Our Lady in the sense that he did not realize how wonderful she was. After she had given birth, he did know her, did see fully who she was. 'Through her Child, she had become lovelier and worthier than the whole world, for she had welcomed into the little home of her womb Him whom the whole world cannot contain.' [57] Secondly, there is a theory that, in the *Catena aurea*, St Thomas attributes to St Hilary. The Israelites could not look at Moses while he was speaking with God, because his face shone with too great a glory (cf. 2 Cor 3:7). Similarly, Joseph could not look upon Mary, could not 'know' her, while she was overshadowed by the 'radiance of the Power of the Most High'. However, after she had given birth, he did know her—'by gazing at her face, not by lustful contact'.[58]

St Thomas says that, before the Annunciation, Mary had not vowed lifelong virginity absolutely, but she did deeply desire it, waiting upon God's will. Once she had accepted Joseph as her husband, the two of them took a vow of virginity.[59] The desire is reflected in Our Lady's response to Gabriel: 'How shall this be done, because I know not man?' In other words: 'How shall this be done, because *I am resolved to be a virgin?*' (cf. Lk 1:34). As Christians, we are not surprised by such a vow-desire. In the light of the gospel of charity, it makes perfect sense, because, as Balthasar says, 'every true love has the inner form of a vow.'[60] In the likeness of the generous love of Christ for His Church, anyone who loves desires to dedicate himself fully and completely, to commit himself for ever to the one he loves. That is why all

[57] ST 3a 28, 3, ad 3, quoting St John Chrysostom, *Opus imperfectum in Matthaeum* [1, 25]; PG 56, 635.

[58] ST 3a 28, 3, ad 3.

[59] Cf. ST 3a 28, 4.

[60] Hans Urs von Balthasar, *The Christian State of Life* (San Francisco, 1983), 39.

Christian life stands under vow—whether of Baptism, Marriage, or the Consecrated Life. However, were we to look at Our Lady's vow with the eyes of her fellow Jews, the desire would be perplexing. Virginity as a permanent state was not generally esteemed in Israel, though among the Essenes there is evidence of a new and more positive attitude emerging.[61] The Jews prized above all else a richly fruitful marriage: the wife like a fruitful vine on the side of the house, the children as olive plants round about the table (cf. Ps 127:3f.). Through his descendants, the Israelite who feared the Lord could look forward to a kind of immortality—even in this world (cf. Ps 127:5f.). As St Thomas says, before Christ was born of the Jews, the men and women of His people had to marry and have children, because the worship of God, the true religion, was spread through physical descent ('secundum carnis originem').[62]

By vowing virginity, Our Lady renounced this beautiful natural fruitfulness. For any human culture, the surrender of the power to transmit life is a kind of spiritual death. For the Jews, it was a folly, a humiliation. Mary of Nazareth embraced both the spiritual death and the humiliation out of love for God, for His Anointed One, and for her people. Pope John Paul II has said that the Holy Virgin wanted to make reparation for the sins of Israel. God had called Daughter Sion to a covenant marriage. He wanted her to be His pure Bride. But, as we learn from the book of the Prophet Hosea, she was regularly unfaithful (cf. Hos 1:2ff.). The later Prophets felt sure that it would not always be so. On the horizon, they discerned a pure dawn, a Virgin Daughter Sion, who would give the Lord a spotless fidelity.

---

[61] Cf. Pope John Paul II's General Audience Address of July 28, 1996 (*L'Osservatore Romano* 31 [1996]: 7).

[62] Cf. ST 3a 28, 4. There is a tradition of periodic and perpetual continence among the Prophets. See 'The Perpetual Virginity of Mary in the Light of Jewish Law and Tradition', in Brother Anthony M. Opisso, *Born of the Ever-Virgin Mary* (Highland, 1995), 12ff.

'Again I will build you,' says Jeremiah, 'and you shall be built, O Virgin Israel' (Jer 31:4). 'For as a young man marries a virgin,' prophesies Isaiah, 'so shall your sons marry you, and as the Bridegroom rejoices over the Bride, so shall your God rejoice over you' (Is 62:5). By the grace of her Immaculate Conception, Our Lady wants to be—and is—that pure Bride. As our Holy Father says:

> Mary is well aware of her people's infidelity, and she wants personally to be a Bride who is faithful to her most beloved divine Spouse.[63]

But if Our Lady vowed virginity, at least in desire, how could she accept betrothal to St Joseph? The answer is simple and beautiful: because it was the will of the Lord God of Israel.[64] As St Thomas says, when he explains why Mary's willingness to be betrothed implies no diminishing of the virginity of her mind:

> We ought to believe that the Blessed Virgin, the Mother of God, by the intimate prompting of the Holy Spirit, was willing to be betrothed, confident that by divine help she would never come to carnal union; still, she entrusted this to the divine will. And so she suffered no harm to her virginity.[65]

By a kind of divine chivalry, the Son of God, with the Father and the Holy Spirit, seeks to guard the honour of His Mother, and so He wills that she should be betrothed to St Joseph. Vir-

---

[63] Address to General Audience, December 4, 1991, no. 6; *Insegnamenti di Giovanni Paolo II* 14/2 (1991): 1310.

[64] Adrienne von Speyr gets to the heart of the matter: '[For Mary] the decision of marriage is not a decision against virginity. . . . She does not reflect on their compatibility. She knows only one rule which she follows without swerving, stopping or turning back: to do the will of God perfectly in everything' (*Handmaid of the Lord* [San Francisco, 1985], 55).

[65] ST 3a 29, 1, ad 1. The consent that makes a true marriage was given by Mary and Joseph. 'Both consented to conjugal union, but not expressly to carnal union, except under the condition that it be pleasing to God' (ibid., 29, 2).

ginity is to be protected by marriage. St Thomas quotes a noble text from another knightly soul—St Ambrose:

> The Lord would rather have had people doubt His origin than the chastity (*pudore*) of His Mother. For He knew how delicate is the modesty of a virgin and how vulnerable the reputation of chastity. He did not want faith in His [Virgin] Birth to be built up at the expense of injury to His Mother.[66]

The Beauty of Humility

Pride is ugly. It inflates and swells, brings disorder and deformity into the soul. Humility, by contrast, is the reassertion of order. St Bernard saw a deep correspondence between the beauty of Our Lady's virginity and the humility of her approach to the Father. The spotless virginity of her body was, in a way, a sacrament of the childlike humility of her soul. According to St Bernard, there was a beautiful mingling ('pulchra permixtio') of virginity and humility in Our Lady; without humility, her virginity would not have pleased God.[67] She was humble of heart, emptied of self and therefore ready to be filled by God. Yes, virginity and humility coincide in this quality that, for want of a better word, the English Catholic writer Caryll Houselander called 'emptiness'.

> It is not a formless emptiness, a void without meaning; on the contrary, it has a shape, a form given to it by the purpose for which it is intended. It is emptiness like the hollow in the reed . . . like the hollow in the cup . . . like that of the bird's nest. . . . The pre-Advent emptiness of Our Lady's purposeful virginity was indeed like those three things. She was a reed through which the Eternal Love was to be piped as a shepherd's song. She was the flowerlike chalice into which the purest water of humanity was to be poured, mingled with wine, changed to the

---

[66] Ibid., ad 2, quoting St Ambrose, *Expositio Evangelii secundum Lucam* 2, 1, 27; PL 15, 1553.

[67] St Bernard, *Sermo 1 in laudibus Virginis Matris*, no. 5; *Sancti Bernardi opera* 4:18.

crimson blood of love, and lifted up in sacrifice. She was the warm nest rounded to the shape of humanity to receive the Divine Little Bird.[68]

Our Lady's virginity is good earth made ready by God to receive the seed of His Word. The Akathist Hymn of the Byzantine Church praises this beautiful receptiveness in the Virgin: 'As a clear and untilled space thou madest the divine Ear of Corn to burst forth; hail, thou living table having space for the Bread of Life.'[69] The world may see virginity or celibacy as something negative, a void. But the Mother of God reveals that it is empty only as everything receptive is empty, as a chalice is empty so it may contain first wine and then the Blood of Christ.

The humility of Our Blessed Lady is childlike. After Jesus, Our Blessed Lady is the most perfect example of that spiritual childhood commended by her Son in the Gospel. St Bonaventure does a Marian gloss on Our Lord's word: 'Whoever humbles himself like this little girl [parvula ista] will be the greatest in the Kingdom of God. Although she was the Mother of God, she wanted to be very little in her own eyes.'[70] In childlikeness of heart, as in everything else, the Mother of God is perfectly conformed to her Son. Address yourselves to her, says Charles Péguy, with confidence, 'to her who is infinitely great, because she is also infinitely small, infinitely humble, a young mother, to her who is infinitely young, because she is also infinitely mother'.[71] From her conception, the Mother of the Son was given the grace of the Holy Spirit in order to be the beloved adopted daughter of the Father and to respond to Him with the humble faith, hope, and love of a child. By the grace that filled her from the beginning, the Blessed Virgin's assent to God's will

---

[68] Caryll Houselander, *The Reed of God* (London, 1945), 1.

[69] Cited by Houselander, *Reed*, 1.

[70] *De Assumptione B. V. M. sermo 4*; 696.

[71] 'Le Porche de la deuxième vertu', in *Oeuvres poétiques complètes* (Paris, 1957), 567f.

is free of the tired old cynicism, the aging arrogance, of the sinner. 'Be it done unto me according to thy word.' In Psalm 130, Mary's ancestor King David gives us a prophecy of her childlike heart: 'O Lord, my heart is not lifted up, my eyes are not raised too high. I do not occupy myself with things too great and too marvellous for me. But I have calmed and quieted my soul, like a child quieted on its mother's breast, like a child that is quieted is my soul' (Ps 130:1f.). In her Yes to God, she is perfectly childlike and openhearted, and now, glorified in body as well as in soul, she enjoys the eternal youth of her Son's Resurrection.[72] The 'spirit of childhood' is not just the romantic ideal of the poets. It is a woman of flesh and blood, an ever-young lady, the Ever-Virgin Mother of God.

Among Catholic writers, no one has praised more tenderly the spiritual childlikeness of Mary than the French novelist Georges Bernanos. In his *Diary of a Country Priest*, the young dying priest is told by his older mentor to turn to the Blessed Mother.

> The eyes of Our Lady are the only real child eyes that have ever been raised to our shame and sadness. Yes, lad, to pray to her properly, you have to feel those eyes of hers upon you. They are not eyes of indulgence—for there is no indulgence without some kind of bitter experience. No, they are eyes of tender compassion, sorrowful surprise, and with something more in them, something inconceivable, inexpressible, something that makes her younger than sin, younger than the race from which

[72] As Péguy says so beautifully: 'And only two bodies have returned from the world/ Intact, pure, girded, fresher than a baby,/ And two bodies have left the sordid round/ Brighter than wheat on harvest eve' ('Suite d'Eve', in *Oeuvres poétiques*, 1479). The eternal youth of the glorified Mary appears in the depiction of her Assumption and Coronation in the left portal of the West Façade of Notre Dame in Paris: 'Two angels, tremulous with respect, lift the Virgin from the tomb. They carry her gently on a long veil, for they dare not touch the sacred body. Jesus raises His hand to bless His Mother, and the Apostles thoughtfully meditate on this mystery. *Mary is beautiful, clothed in eternal youth; age does not approach her*' (Mâle, *Religious Art in France*, 251ff.).

she sprang, and though a mother, by grace Mother of All Graces, the youngest sister of the human race.[73]

What is true of the natural order applies also, by the mercy of God, to the supernatural order. When we are incorporated into Christ in Baptism, we become sons-in-the-Son—children of His heavenly Father, but also children of His human Mother. This is Our Blessed Lord's gift to us from the Cross: 'Behold your Mother' (cf. Jn 19:27). Now, the wonderful thing about this dear Mother of ours is that she is more childlike than her children, and the object of her motherly mediation in Heaven is to make us more childlike—to help us be more obedient and receptive to God's will, to be more open to the Spirit of the Son, who wants to cry in our hearts, 'Abba, Father' (cf. Gal 4:6). By her life on earth, Our Lady is our model for childlike humility; by her intercession in Heaven, she is also its mediatrix. If we want to convert and become like little children, it is to Mary that we should turn.

Pristine Faith

The Blessed Virgin was not passively deployed by God. No, she freely cooperated with the work of our salvation through her faith and loving obedience. This cooperation began at the Annunciation when she said Yes to the God the Son's becoming incarnate from her by the Holy Spirit, and it continued all the way to the Cross and the Empty Tomb.

The cooperative Yes of Our Lady is beautiful, first of all, because it reveals the infinite courtesy of God the Father. He does not impose His Son on mankind. Why, asks St Thomas Aquinas, was the Incarnation preceded by an announcement? He answers:

> To show that a kind of spiritual marriage was taking place between the Son of God and human nature. And so, through the

[73] Georges Bernanos, *Oeuvres romanesques* (Paris, 1961), 1194.

Annunciation, the consent of the Virgin was sought in the name of all human nature.[74]

Like the Fathers, St Thomas sees the Hypostatic Union as a nuptial mystery: God the Son marries human nature to Himself in the Virgin's womb. Now it is consent that makes a marriage, and so human nature had to pledge itself through the faith and obedience of the Blessed Virgin. As St Augustine and St Leo said, she conceived the Word in her mind in faith before conceiving Him in her womb in flesh.[75] In one of his sermons 'in praise of the Virgin Mother', St Bernard pictures all the Patriarchs in Limbo, every man on earth, every creature in the cosmos, breathless with excitement, waiting for the Virgin to say the Yes that will enable the Son of God to enter human nature to redeem us.[76]

Our Lady's cooperation with our redemption is also beautiful because it is an act of pristine Christian faith. Hers is the fairest and freshest faith of all. She is the first to believe. The believing Church exists in Mary before a single Apostle has been called. The Church's supreme model of faith is not Peter the Pope or Stephen the Deacon, but Mary, the lowly Handmaid of the Lord. This faith is unspoilt, unreserved, a total gift of self, the abandonment of a child to her Father.

Finally, Our Lady's cooperative Yes is beautiful, because it is a cooperation with the incarnate Son's restoration of mankind to the beauty of deifying grace.

The Lady of Fair Weeping

Angelico shows the Mother with the Son in His childhood on her lap, but in the superimposed Crucifixion, he shows her with Him in His adulthood on the Cross. The grave angels by her

---

[74] ST 3a 30, 1.

[75] Cf. St Augustine, *Sermo 215*, 4; PL 38, 1074; St Leo, *Tractatus 21*, 1; CCSL 138, 86.

[76] *Sermo 4 in laudibus Virginis Matris*, no. 8; 53f.

throne are already pointing towards Calvary, for they carry the instruments of the Passion.

The paradox of the theological aesthetic is that the supreme revelation of the beauty of the Trinity takes place in the crucified form of the Son. No one shares more deeply than Our Lady in the Passion, and so none knows more sharply the paradox of its beauty. Our Lady, as Francis Thompson said, is 'the lady of fair weeping'.[77] No created person is more beautiful than she, yet none has borne more pain. St Antoninus lets us hear her lament:

> 'The angel said that I was blessed among women, but now I am unhappier than all women. . . . No mother felt so much pain in childbirth as I now feel in the Passion of Christ.' . . . When she saw her Son with the crown of thorns that Pilate's soldiers fixed on His head, and that face, beautiful above the sons of men, flowing with blood from the piercing thorns and befouled by spittle, when she saw Him unable through lassitude to bear the Cross on His shoulders, she might have said, 'Who will grant me to die for thee, my Son? O my Son, not just the light of my eyes but the glory of all peoples. . . .'[78]

The Blessed Virgin is the lady of *fair* weeping. Her tears are beautiful. These are the sorrows of one who is all-beautiful, fully free from the deformity of sin. Those affected by Original Sin tend to build walls between themselves and the sufferings of others. (The walls get rationalized as a 'thick skin' or a 'stiff upper lip'.) We can be blind to evil, whether moral or physical. But in Mary Immaculate no sinful self-absorption blocks out the world's woes, and no foolish fantasies disguise the foulness of sin. No lamentation has been lovelier, no compassion purer, less marred by self-pity. The sinless Spirit-filled heart of Mary is beautifully centred on the will of the Father and on His and her Son and those for whom He suffers. With a keenness unmatched

---

[77] 'The Lady of fair weeping,/ At the garden's core,/ Sang a song of sweet and sore/ And the after-sleeping' ('The Mistress of Vision', *The Poems of Francis Thompson*, new ed. [London, 1913], 181).

[78] St Antoninus, *Summae sacrae theologiae*, 379ff.

by any sinner's, Our Lady feels, with Jesus and for us, the assault of pain and even more the attack of sin.

Mary is not just a Mother who is sorrowful because her Son is suffering. Standing at the foot of the Cross, Our Blessed Lady does not passively or even just patiently assist at the Sacrifice of her Son. In obedience to the Father's saving will, she gives up His and her Son. She gives, she offers; she does not merely let go. With love, she says Yes to the immolation of the Victim who is flesh of her flesh, the fruit of her womb. St Albert says that Our Lady joined herself to the Father of mercies in His greatest work of mercy when she shared in the Passion of her Son and 'thus became the helper of our redemption and the Mother of our spiritual generation'.[79] According to St Antoninus, she stands by the Cross in devotion (*pietas*) not only towards her natural Son but also towards her adopted sons, for by her consent she is cooperating with their redemption.[80] To describe the beauty of Our Lady's cooperation with her Son's saving work, some of the Popes of our century have called Our Blessed Lady 'Co-Redemptrix'.[81] It is a long and daunting Latin word, but its meaning is summed up in one syllable of Anglo-Saxon—the word that is the true heart of Mary: *Yes*. No word is lovelier when uttered to God's glory, no reality more efficacious. Saying Yes to God is coredemptive.

The Silent Sabbath

The Yes of Our Lady does not end on Good Friday with the Great Cry and the yielding of the spirit. Fra Angelico shows this beautifully in the *Entombment*, which was once the central panel

---

[79] *Mariale sive quaestiones super Evangelium Missus est*, q. 29, no. 3; *Beati Alberti Magni opera omnia*, vol. 37 (Paris, 1898), 62.

[80] Cf. St Antoninus, *Summae sacrae*, 379.

[81] For a review of the teaching, see J. A. Schug and M. I. Miravalle, 'Mary, Co-Redemptrix: The Significance of her Title in the Magisterium of the Church', in M. I. Miravalle, ed., *Co-Redemptrix, Mediatrix, Advocate: Theological Foundations: Towards a Papal Definition?* (Santa Barbara, 1995), 215–46.

The Entombment. Panel from the predella of the San Marco altarpiece.

in the predella of the altarpiece. Joseph of Arimathea supports the lifeless body, while Mary bows low and kisses the Saviour's hand, an act of purest reverence.

The faith and love of Our Lady last into Holy Saturday. The dead body of the Son of God lies in the tomb, while His soul descends into Sheol, the Limbo of the Fathers. Jesus goes down into the hideous kingdom of death to proclaim the power of the Cross and the coming victory of the Resurrection and to open Heaven's gates to Adam and Eve and all the souls of the just. The Apostles, hopeless and forlorn, know none of this. 'As yet', St John tells us, 'they did not know the Scripture, that He must rise from the dead' (Jn 20:9). In all Israel, is there no faith in Jesus? On this silent Saturday, this terrible Shabbat, while the Jews' true Messiah sleeps the sleep of death, who burns the lights of hope? Is there no loyal remnant? There is, and its name is Mary. In the fortitude of faith, she keeps the Sabbath candles alight for her Son. That is why Saturday, the sacred day of her physical brethren, is Our Lady's weekly festival. On the first Holy Saturday, in the person of Mary of Nazareth, Israel, now an unblemished Bride, faces her hardest trial and, through the fortitude of the Holy Spirit, is triumphant.

Maria Assumpta

The body of the Immaculate Virgin was for nine months the shrine of Divine Beauty, the palace of the King of Glory. It is, therefore, right and fitting that, at the end of her earthly course, she should be taken up by her Son to share, in body as well as soul, in His risen beauty. As St John Damascene says in his Canon for the Dormition, addressing the Holy Virgin herself:

> Life arose from thee without destroying the seals of thy virginity. How then could the spotless tabernacle of thy body, the source of life, become a partaker of death? [82]

[82] *Canon in Dormitionem* 3; PG 96, 1365A.

St Bonaventure applies to *Maria Assumpta* a text of Wisdom (7:29): 'She is more beautiful than the sun, and above all the order of the stars; being compared with the light, she is found before it.' Yes, says Bonaventure, the Blessed Virgin is truly more beautiful than the sun, *serenissima*, lovelier than the bluest of unclouded skies. She is more beautiful than the sun because she is closer to the fount of all beauty and with a greater disposition to receive its waters of perfect beauty. The Virgin Mary, shining above the sun and stars, has been made like 'the beautiful and delicate Trinity'.[83]

Mary, *tota pulchra*, is also *spes nostra*. It is for God's glory, but also for man's good, that the Mother of the God-Man is made so beautiful. As Father Vincent McNabb, O.P., once wrote:

> This lady, in her loveliness fair as the moon, and in her strength 'terrible as an army in battle array', is one of God's consummate mercies to men. There is nothing in all her beauty of body and soul that is not a gift, and an acknowledged gift, of God. Yet each gift of God to her was part of the riches of His mercy to us.[84]

In the purity of her whole person on earth, and in the glory of her whole person in Heaven, the Mother of God is the Church's image and beginning, the promise of final beauty for the members of Christ. What she is now, the Church is meant to be and one day will be. The Woman clothed with the sun and crowned with the stars is both Mary and the Church: the Church in Mary and Mary in the Church.[85]

---

[83] Cf. *De Assumptione B. V. M. sermo 2*; 9:691.

[84] Vincent McNabb, O.P., *Mary of Nazareth* (London, 1939), xiv.

[85] St Methodius of Olympus sees the Woman in the twelfth chapter of Revelation as the Church beautified in the resurrection of the flesh. Quoting Isaiah 60:4 ('All thy sons have come from afar, and thy daughters shall rise up at thy side'), he says: 'It is the Church whose children by Baptism will swiftly come running to her from all sides after the resurrection. She rejoices to receive the light that never sets, clothed as she is in the brightness of the Word as with a robe.... [She] gleams in pure and wholly unsullied and

Once, in faith on earth, Our Lady cooperated with her Son in His acquiring of the divine beauty of grace for us through His Passion. Now, in vision in Heaven, in the glory of body and soul, she cooperates with Him in the distribution of that grace. The living waters of the Holy Spirit flow from the Father and the Son through the Son's pierced Heart and along the 'aqueduct' of the Mother's prayers.[86] By God's will, no lovely gift comes to us except through the hands of Mary.[87] She is the Mediatrix of All Graces, the Mediatrix of the Beauty of Christ.

2. Marian Devotion and the Civilization of Love

The Anti-Culture of Anti-Christ

Where true devotion to the Blessed Virgin thrives, so does Christian culture. When true devotion dies, so does Christian culture. Our Lady is the model and protective Mother of what the Popes of our times have called the 'Civilization of Love', the Mediatrix of all beauty, the Queen of all the arts.

There can be no Christian culture without Christ, but without true devotion to the Mother, true faith in the Son soon withers. As Cardinal Newman saw in the last century, the Reformation's Maryless Christology developed, in Liberal Protestantism, into a Christless Christianity. Even in Newman's lifetime, the denominations that had thrown off devotion to the Mother

---

abiding beauty, emulating the brilliance of the lights' (*Symposium* 8, 5; PG 18, 145CD).

[86] The image of the 'aqueduct' is that of St Bernard (cf. *Sermo in Nativitate Beatae Mariae* [*De aquaeductu*]; *Sancti Bernardi opera*, ed. J. Leclercq and H. Rochais, vol. 5 [Rome, 1968], 275ff.).

[87] Cf. St Bernard, *In vigilia Nativitatis Domini sermo 3*, 10; *Sancti Bernardi opera*, 4:219. Cf. St Bonaventure, *In Nativitate Domini sermo 1*, 1; *Sancti Bonaventurae opera omnia* 9:103.

had begun to tolerate doubt about the Son—His true divinity, His virginal conception, and His bodily Resurrection.

> For if Mary's glory is so very great, how cannot His be greater still who is the Lord and God of Mary? He is infinitely above His Mother; and all that grace which filled her is but the overflowings and superfluities of His incomprehensible Sanctity. And history teaches us the same lesson. Look at the Protestant countries which threw off all devotion to her three centuries ago, under the notion that to put her from their thoughts would be exalting the praises of her Son. Has that consequence really followed from their profane conduct towards her? Just the reverse—the countries, Germany, Switzerland, England, which so acted, have in great measure ceased to worship Him, and have given up their belief in His Divinity; while the Catholic Church, wherever she is to be found, adores Christ as true God and true Man, as firmly as she ever did; and strange indeed would it be, if it ever happened otherwise.[88]

The Theotokos—by her name and her icon, by her lovely person and her loving prayers—is the God-given protection of the truth about her Son. As it was in antiquity, so it is again in modernity: the Blessed Virgin crushes all the serpents of heresy ('cunctas haereses sola interemisti in universo mundo'). Henri de Lubac has shown how the 'atheistic humanists' of the last one hundred and fifty years have been not only a-theistic and anti-theistic but anti-Christian, anti-Christ.[89] It is above all God

---

[88] John Henry Newman, *Meditations and Devotions*, new ed. (London, 1964), 145.

[89] Cf. Henri de Lubac, *The Drama of Atheistic Humanism* (San Francisco, 1995), 12. See also Ferdinand Ulrich, *Atheismus und Menschwerdung*, new ed. (Einsiedeln, 1975), passim. Paul Claudel remembered a fever of anti-Christ sentiment in the years of his early manhood: 'I take myself back again in thought to that sinister period of 1890 to 1910, in which my youth and maturity were spent, a period of aggressive and triumphant materialism and scepticism, dominated by the figure of Ernest Renan. What efforts then were made to obscure the divinity of Christ, to veil that unendurable face, to flatten the Christian fact, to efface its contours beneath the tangled bandages of erudition

incarnate whom they will not worship. The creature intent on glorifying itself resents the Creator who humbled Himself. That is why some theologians of the Tradition have suggested that Lucifer's sin was directed from the beginning against the Incarnation.[90] St Augustine understood this mentality. He confesses that, before his conversion, he was too proud to accept the God who made Himself small—the baby in the womb and the arms of Mary.[91]

Our Lady protects mankind from the anti-human anti-culture of the Anti-Christ. She leads us to the God-Man, who invites us into the heavenly city of humility and saves us from the Man of Sin, who inveigles us into the hellish city of pride. When the Virgin Mother is not venerated, the Son's self-emptying is soon forgotten, and men dream of Progress, Superman, and the Will to Power. Mary's womb and heart proclaim what Prometheanism cannot bear to hear: the humility of the

---

and doubt!' ('La photographie du Christ', in *Oeuvres complètes de Paul Claudel*, vol. 28, *Commentaires et exégèses* 10 [Paris, 1978], 291f.).

[90] Suarez, for example, argued that Lucifer's pride is only comprehensible on the supposition that the future Incarnation of the Word was revealed to him when he was *in via*. He refused to obey a created will, even one existing in an uncreated Person. His pride is directed, therefore, from the beginning, against the humility of God in becoming man (*De malis angelis* in *Opera omnia*, new ed., vol. 7 [Paris, 1857], 986). This is a problematic thesis, not least because of what it implies about the predestination of the Incarnation. However, the point Suarez is making about the specifically anti-Christ hatred of Satan remains valid.

[91] 'I was not yet humble enough to hold the humble Jesus as my God, nor did I know what lesson His embracing of our weakness was to teach. . . . [Your Word] built for Himself here below a humble house of clay. His intention was to bring down from themselves and bring up to Himself those to be made subject to Him. He wanted to heal the swollenness of their pride and nurture their love, so that they should no longer march forward in self-confidence but might realize their weakness when they saw the Deity at their feet, enfeebled by the taking of our coat of human nature. Then, weary at last, they would cast themselves down upon His humanity, and when it rose, so would they' (*Confessiones* 7, 18; CCSL 27, 108).

Creator in becoming incarnate and the humility of the creature in welcoming Him.[92] As Balthasar says:

> Mary's life must be regarded as the prototype of what the *ars Dei* can fashion from a human material which puts up no resistance to him. It is a feminine life which, in any case more than masculine life, awaits being shaped by the man, the bridegroom, Christ, and God. It is a virginal life which desires no other formative principle but God and the fruit which God gives it to bear, to give birth to, to nourish and to rear. It is at the same time a maternal and a bridal life whose power of surrender reaches from the physical to the highest spiritual level. In all this it is simply a life that lets God dispose of it as he will.[93]

It is this Marian attitude towards God that, ever since the Enlightenment, the ideologies of modernity have fought to destroy. The attack by David Strauss and the Hegelians of the Left on the historicity of the Virginal Conception, and Liberal Protestantism's capitulation to that attack, can be seen, therefore, as the decisive turning point in the war of Promethean and Dionysian atheism against the Christian culture of Europe.[94] If man is to soar upwards to self-fulfilment, then, at all costs, God's

---

[92] See Ulrich on 'The Virgin and the Ever-Greater God', in *Atheismus*, 67ff.

[93] H 1, 542; GL 1, 564.

[94] In his monograph masterpiece (*Conceição virginal de Jesus. Análise crítica de pesquisa liberal protestante, desde a 'Declaração de Eisenach' até hoje, sobre o testemunho de Mt. 1. 18–25 e Lc 1. 26–38* [Rome, 1980]), José de Freitas Ferreira has charted the collapse of orthodox Christian belief in the Virginal Conception within Protestantism from the Eisenach Declaration of 1892 to the theologies of today. He shows how the arguments of Liberal Protestantism against the historicity of the Virginal Conception are in every age merely the turgid restatement of Strauss's position. The denial is sustained by intellectual 'lethargy' and 'philosophical a priorism', that is to say, a rationalist prejudice against revealed religion and the miraculous. In the case of Strauss himself, de Freitas Ferreira proves his uncritical debt to Hegel: 'It is Hegel who furnishes him with the definitive semantic key to the Scriptures enabling him to distinguish between the religious concept and its image or sensible expression. Both are inseparable, but the one true object of faith, the perennial and timeless reality, is not the historical and sensible dimension of the biblical narrative (for example, miracles) but its religious–doctrinal content' (273f.).

descent to a lowly womb must be denied. The nineteenth century closes with Nietzsche-Zarathustra's demand for deicide:
'To you, Higher Men, this God was your greatest danger.' Only
when the humble God is dead can the Superman arise.[95]

The Beauty of Beholding

True devotion to the Blessed Virgin builds up the Civilization of
Love because it leads men into the admiration and contemplation that fill her heart, the admiration without which there is no
love, the contemplation without which there is no civilization.

The great German Catholic philosopher Josef Pieper has argued that leisure is the basis of human culture.[96] By 'leisure' he
means, not procrastination, but contemplation. He compares
and contrasts the two powers of the human mind as distinguished by the Schoolmen: *ratio* and *intellectus*. The first is discursive activity, the mind examining and searching, arguing and
defining. The second is contemplative rest, the mind simply and
effortlessly gazing upon the truth. The two operate together in
our knowledge in this world, but there is no doubt that the
second is the higher of the two. Discursive reason is properly
human, but there is something superhuman about contemplative intuition. In Heaven, Thomas and Bonaventure no longer
argue and deduce, but they rest and they see, they see and they
love, they love and they praise.[97]

Pieper argues that, since the Enlightenment, discursive reason
has been exalted, while contemplation has been despised. For
Kant, all thought is discursive. Philosophy is work—hard, Prussian
toil. Anything effortless is to be despised. By contrast, St Thomas

---

[95] 'Vom höheren Menschen', *Also sprach Zarathustra*, vol. 2 of *Werke*, ed. K. Schlechta (Munich, 1966), 522f.

[96] *Leisure, the Basis of Culture* (London, 1952).

[97] 'Ibi vacabimus et videbimus, videbimus et amabimus, amabimus et lauda-bimus. Ecce quod erit in fine sine fine' (*De civitate Dei* 22, 30; CCSL 48, 866).

insists that the highest moral good is characterized by effortlessness, that playfulness is a virtue and too little play a vice, and that, for the perfection of human society, it is necessary for some men to devote their lives to contemplation.[98] There are, of course, degrees of such beholding: the natural wonder of the child, the philosopher, and the poet; the mystic's gazing on the Lord with eyes of faith and love; the face-to-face beholding of the Trinity by the blessed. But, in each case, the higher takes up and perfects the lower.[99]

There is no culture, then, without contemplative wonder at the beauty of being. Now this natural attitude is perfected supernaturally and most perfectly in Our Lady, who magnifies the Lord for His marvels (cf. Lk 1:46) and ponders the things of Jesus in her heart (cf. Lk 2:51). It is the Virgin Mary, even more than Martha's sister, who 'hath chosen the best part' (cf. Lk 10:42). This is a major motif in Angelico's art. For example, in the San Marco *Deposition from the Cross*, Our Lady kneels, hands clasped, her head bowed, her eyes fixed on the scarlet wounds. Again, in the great Annunciations of San Marco and Cortona, she is pure openness to God: her eyes on the angel, her ears receiving the Word. Yes, she is *pure* in her openness and therefore perfect in her contemplation. The gazing at divine beauty is itself a beautiful act, for which the spiritual beauty of chastity is an essential requirement: the man whose reason is clouded by concupiscence cannot see clearly.[100] No human person is purer than the Immaculate, so none is more suited to contemplation. Her active cooperation with God is the fruit of her contemplative openness to Him. Her *fiat* was the most fruitful act of any created person, for, through it, the uncreated person of the Word took flesh for our salvation; and yet it is not a masculine initia-

[98] Cf. Pieper, *Leisure*, 33ff.

[99] In ST 2a2ae 180, 4, ad 3, St Thomas explains Richard of St Victor's six kinds of contemplation.

[100] Cf. ST 2a2ae 180, 2, ad 3.

tive but a feminine response, a welcoming of the Word in the womb. At the Annunciation, it is not masterful manly enterprise that God asks of mankind, but humble womanly receptivity.

God made the human mind to be Mary-like. According to St Thomas, the core of the human mind is openness, receptivity to reality. This is the 'possible intellect', the capacity to admit into oneself the forms of all things. It is not strictly by the busy agent intellect that man understands, but by the receptive possible intellect.[101] We can call this Marian centre of our minds 'passive' so long as we remember that, in its receptivity, it undergoes no dwindling or damaging of its natural properties. It receives the act to which it was in potency yet loses nothing of what it is.[102] There is, we might say, a kind of *virginity* about the natural function of the human mind. Certainly, true wisdom comes, not through thrusting 'curiosity', but by humble studiousness, the handmaidenly service of the truth.[103]

Balthasar argues that, when true devotion to Our Lady weakens, the feminine-contemplative heart of human culture is forgotten, and male activism and Utilitarianism reign supreme.

> Without Mariology, Christianity threatens imperceptibly to become inhuman. The Church becomes functionalistic, soulless, a hectic enterprise without any point of rest, estranged from its true nature by the planners. And, because in this manly-masculine world, all that we have is one ideology replacing another, everything becomes polemical, critical, bitter, humourless, and ultimately boring, and people in their masses run away from such a Church.[104]

Woman, said Gertrud von Le Fort, is 'the guardian of culture'.[105] She is indeed—through the example and mediation of *the* Woman, the Virgin Mother of God.

[101] Cf. *Quaestio disputata de anima* 1, 3, sed contra.
[102] Cf. ST 1a 79, 2.
[103] Ibid., 166, q. 166.
[104] Balthasar, 'The Marian Principle', *Elucidations* (London, 1975), 72.
[105] Cf. *Die Krone der Frau* (Zurich, 1952), 78.

Blessed Art Thou among Women

When he is speaking of the Incarnation, St Paul says that the Son of God is 'born of woman' (cf. Gal 4:4). The word 'woman' is significant. For the Apostle, as for Jesus Himself at Cana (cf. Jn 2:4) and from the Cross (cf. 19:26), the Virgin Mary is *the* Woman of human history, the New Eve, the woman whose crushing of the serpent was prophesied by Moses (cf. Gen 3:15). This woman, this humble Virgin of Israel, stands at the centre of Divine Revelation, for the Father's revealing Word becomes man in her flesh and through her faith. She, therefore, 'attains a union with God that exceeds all the expectations of the human spirit'.[106] The highest elevation of human nature took place in the masculine gender, when the Divine Person of the Son of God became man and male. But the highest elevation of the human person took place in the feminine gender, in the Virgin Mother of God. Her divine maternity gives her a dignity far beyond the highest of the angels: she is more honourable than the Cherubim, incomparably more glorious than the Seraphim. The only truly fulfilled human person, the only one already glorified by Christ in body as well as soul, is not a male but a female. The greatest after God is a woman.

'Blessed art thou among women': blessed above all her sisters, yet blessed also on their behalf. All womanhood is made radiant by the shining Theotokos. When the Virgin Mary is humbly honoured for the sake of her Son, women will be honoured, and human culture will have a firm foundation in the sexual order of the Creator. Far from oppressing women, orthodox Catholic doctrine about and devotion to Our Lady have revealed the true beauty of womanhood. A simple English carol from the last years of the Catholic Middle Ages expresses this magnificently. It is one of several that present the excellence of

---

[106] Cf. *Mulieris dignitatem*, no. 3.

the Mother of God as the grounds for courtesy towards all women. 'Women be both good and true, Witness on Mary.' [107] It is a down-to-earth Englishman's grateful celebration, in the light of the Virgin, of mothers and daughters, of sisters and wives. Something similar can be seen in the fifteenth-century ballad of Robin Hood, much loved by Chesterton:

> A good manner then had Robin;
> In land where that he were,
> Every day ere he would dine
> Three Masses would he hear.
>
> The one is the worship of the Father,
> And another of the Holy Ghost,
> The third of our dear Lady
> That he loved all the most.
>
> Robin loved our dear Lady;
> For fear of deadly sin
> Would he never do company harm
> That any woman was in. [108]

The men and women of the Middle Ages did not always live up to this noble vision. An ugly countertradition of misogyny, with its roots in pagan antiquity, [109] often forces its way to the surface in the Patristic and medieval periods. [110] For example (the most notorious example), in *Corbaccio*, Boccaccio flings out an invective against women and their 'thousand foul passions'. He perversely applies the Scholastic principle *operari sequitur esse*

---

[107] Cited in my article 'Thanks for the Feminine', in C. M. Kelly, ed., *The Enemy Within: Radical Feminism in the Christian Churches* (Milton Keynes, 1992), 127.

[108] 'A Gest of Robyn Hode', in J. Kinsley, ed., *The Oxford Book of Ballads* (Oxford, 1969), 421. Cf. Chesterton, *Chaucer*, 263f.

[109] See, for example, Juvenal, *Satire* 6.

[110] Cf. Alcuin Blamires, *Women Defamed and Women Defended: An Anthology of Medieval Texts* (Oxford, 1992).

The Mocking of Christ.

to women: 'No woman *is* intelligent, therefore no woman can *operate* intelligently.'[111] The eleventh-century poet-bishop Marbod of Rennes appears to trumpet both condemnation and commendation: Woman, as *meretrix*, as whore, is 'the unhappy source, evil root, and corrupt offshoot, bringing to birth every kind of outrage throughout the world', while, as *matrona*, as godly matron, there is nothing better or more beautiful.[112]

The devotion to Mary, whenever it was true, worked against the defamation of woman, wherever it was tried. There was a deep and general sense in the Middle Ages that in the uniquely graced Blessed Virgin all womanhood is raised up to a dignity beyond compare. The Mother of God was everywhere regarded as the perfection of femininity, 'the new beginning', as Pope John Paul II has said in our own time, 'of the dignity and vocation of women'.[113] The radiance of the New Eve shines upon every daughter of the Old. Angelico shows this with sweet courtesy. The penitent Magdalen bears the name, but also some of the beauty, of the sinless Madonna. For example, in the *Mocking of Christ*,[114] she wears the mantle, and imitates the meditation, of the Blessed Mother, and, in the *Deposition*,[115] the purity of Mary of Magdala's kiss is a gift bestowed through Mary of Nazareth's prayer.

The immaculate beauty of Mary challenges men to love and look upon women in a more than merely erotic way. True Marian devotion initiates a man into the chivalry of the gos-

---

[111] Corbaccio, new ed. (Milan, 1988), 285.

[112] *Liber decem capitulorum*, cap. 3 and 4; PL 171, 1698B–1702A. The misogyny is not as crass or as contradictory as it seems. The Bishop's argument would seem to be that, precisely since there is nothing better than womanhood, nothing is worse when it is corrupted (*corruptio optimi pessima*).

[113] *Mulieris dignitatem*, no. 11.

[114] Cell 7. There is some disagreement about the identity of the female saint in this painting. Is it the Virgin, or is it the Magdalen? My view is that it is both: the Magdalen under (literally) the mantle of the Virgin.

[115] In the hall of the Hospice at San Marco.

pel.[116] It is a Christ-given remedy against the threefold concupiscence,[117] an instrument of the cauterizing fire of the Holy Spirit, purging away the dross of male pride and lust. Turning to their spiritual Mother helps men to be small and therefore strong, small like her in themselves, strong like her in the Spirit of the Father and the Son. Devotion to Our Lady has not been tried and found wanting; it has not been properly tried. The Reformation cut it short, and Europe, the world, has ever since been paying a terrible price.

In the Middle Ages, the healing influence of devotion to Our Lady was starting to be felt. There was a place for women. The Mother of God was mediating to men and women a sense of the 'feminine genius'.[118] For the bridal love of the Prince of Heaven, Etheldreda and Frideswide resisted the potentates of the world. A peasant girl, Joan of Arc, took up the sword for the truth of Christ and the honour of France, shaming the lies of the greybeards. In the service of incarnate Wisdom, the abbess Hildegard excelled as musician, physician, metaphysician, theologian, and prophetess. Gertrude, the Mechthilds, and Lady Julian received revelations from the Heart of Jesus. Ever faithful to the Lamb, Birgitta of Sweden and Catherine of Siena, widow-

---

[116] The courtly love tradition may have received some of the healing and ordering influence of devotion to Our Lady. As Fr Kenelm Foster, O.P., has written: 'When all is said, courtly love was an effort to bring sex into harmony with the spirit; it was an aspiration to refinement and, as such, part of that general aspiration towards intellectual, emotional and spiritual refinement which marked the wonderful century in which it was born—the century of St Bernard and the Victorines, of Abelard and the school of Chartres. In this context courtly love becomes intelligible. Let us agree to call it a heresy of a sort; but there were elements in it that cannot be dismissed as merely pagan' ('Courtly Love and Christianity', in *The Two Dantes and Other Studies* [London, 1977], 36).

[117] *Mulieris dignitatem*, no. 10.

[118] See my daughter's study of the 'new feminism' of Pope John Paul II in relation to contemporary Italian society: Helena M. Saward, *La moderna donna ed il suo cattolicesimo: verso il genio femminile* (unpublished dissertation, University of Bristol, 1997).

queen and virgin-daughter of a dyer, corrected, even com-
manded, His Vicars. In the lifetime of Fra Angelico, Christine
de Pizan (1364–1430) wrote an exhilarating Mary-centred
paean of womanhood in *L'Epistre au Dieu d'amours*.[119] 'All this
tempered male authority', says Jack Scarisbrick, 'and . . . asserted
the dignity of womanhood.'[120]

In and through Mary, Jesus gave the women saints of the
Middle Ages (and every age) the privilege of loving Him as
Husband with the heart of a Bride and as Child with the heart
of a Mother.[121] By the advantage of their nature, raised up by
the grace of the Holy Spirit, women express more perfectly
than men the bridal and motherly disposition of Our Lady and
the Church. (That is why women alone, not men, can be consecrated as virgins.)[122] Only when they follow the Beloved Disciple and take Mary into the home of their hearts will men
attain a spousal knowledge of the Bridegroom. It is through
filial love for the Mother that the male soul learns the secret of
bridal love for the Son.[123]

With the Reformation the Marian new beginning for
women was halted. The beauty of medieval Mariology was re-

[119] See Blamires, *Women Defamed*, 283f., for selected passages from Christine's writings.

[120] *The Reformation and the English People* (Oxford, 1984), 171.

[121] I am indebted for this insight to Father François Léthel, O.C.D.: 'The
Church is composed of men and women, who are all called to live this great
mystery of love, but it is evident that woman is privileged in the Church in her
love for Jesus the God-Man, privileged to love Jesus the Child with a mother's
heart, privileged to love Jesus the Bridegroom with the heart of a bride'
(*Théologie de l'amour de Jésus: Ecrits sur la théologie des saints* [Venasque, 1996],
62).

[122] See Marie Thérèse Huguet, *Miryam et Israël: Le mystère de l'Epouse* (Paris,
1987), 91.

[123] I am thinking here of some words of the Holy Father: 'In the context of
the "great mystery" of Christ and of the Church, all are called to respond—*as
a bride*—with the gift of their lives to the inexpressible gift of the love of
Christ, who alone, as the Redeemer of the world, is the Church's Bridegroom'
(*Mulieris dignitatem*, no. 27).

jected, while the ugliness of medieval misogyny remained. John Knox would not sing 'Hail Mary', but he willingly sounded *The First Blast of the Trumpet against the Monstrous Regiment of Women.* The reason why the Protestant denominations have been so vulnerable to feminism is that official Protestantism has refused to recognize the unique role of woman, of *the* Woman, the Mother of God, in the salvation of mankind. Detached from Mary, the Church is no longer seen as a person, a woman, Christ's Bride, and our Mother, but as an organization, a conspiracy of interfering clergymen. In England the Reformation was from the beginning a blow against the dignity of woman. First, Henry VIII discarded his lawful wedded wife for another woman, whom later he had killed. Then he dissolved the nunneries and monasteries, including the abbey and shrine at Walsingham, and allowed Our Lady's lovely image, which he had earlier venerated as a barefoot pilgrim, to be cast into the flames. These combined actions were an attack on the Woman and every woman, on the Mother and every mother, the first blow in a war against chastity, marriage, and the family, which still rages around us. This is England's permanent Civil War, and it will end only when once more she rejoices to be the Dowry of Our Lady.

Conclusion

A few years before the death of Fra Angelico, François Villon graduated as a Master of Arts of the University of Paris. He was a wild man, very different from the mild Dominican painter—a boozer, bandit, and jailbird. He is also France's greatest medieval poet and the author of one of the world's tenderest Marian poems, the *Ballade of Our Lady*, which he wrote in the person of his own poor mother. In it he expresses the true faith in which he wants to live and die and casts himself in complete confidence on the Mother of Mercy. Here a true Christian culture shows its Marian centre.

Villon reveals to us the pastoral power of devotion to Our Lady, the power, that is, of the Mother of the Good Shepherd to touch the hearts of the most erring sheep. For him, the sinless beauty of the Virgin was not a chilling frost but a cheering fire, the hearth of hope. One of the sad effects of Original Sin on our intellects is that we tend to glamourize sin. We think of it as a cheerful solidarity, while we picture sanctity as solemn superiority. But in fact holiness unites, while wickedness separates. Mortal sin is misery, but Sanctifying Grace is always joy (*charis, chara*). It is the sin of pride that cuts a man off, that deadens his heart to the feelings of his fellows. By contrast, she who is full of grace is all charity, bound to her fellow men more closely than they could ever be to themselves. She hurries through the hills to her cousin. Her immaculate heart senses the smallest needs of men: 'They have no wine' (Jn 2:3). She wants to rescue her brethren from the suicide of sin and so lets her Son plunge her into coredemptive com-passion. She takes the Disciple for her son and prays with the Apostles. Our Lady is the purest and fairest of human persons and therefore the kindest and humblest of all. The Immaculate is the Refuge of Sinners.

Through Our Lady, the Holy Spirit draws to Christ and the Father not only gentle souls like the Angelic Friar of Fiesole but also turbulent souls like the Bacchic Poet of Paris. Here is the secret of the beauty of holiness: it attracts, it does not repel. The eyes of Our Lady are not indulgent. Towards a sin they flash with incandescent indignation, terrible as an army in battle order: 'This sin drove nails into the body of my Son.' But towards a sinner the eyes of Our Lady glow with intercessory encouragement: 'The Father's boundless mercy flows from the wounds of my Son.'

To Our Lady, then, in Villon's words, let us with confidence commend our struggle towards the beauty of holiness.

Dame du ciel, régente térrienne . . .

Lady of heaven and earth, and therewithal,
  Crowned Empress of the nether clefts of Hell,
I, thy poor Christian, on thy name do call,
  Commending me to thee, with thee to dwell,
  Albeit in nought I be commendable . . .
O excellent Virgin Princess! Thou didst bear
  King Jesus, our most excellent Comforter,
Who even of this our weakness craved a share
  And for our sake stooped to us from on high,
Offering to death His young life sweet and fair.
Such as He is, Our Lord, I Him declare,
  And in this faith I choose to live and die.[124]

[124] *Rossetti's Poems and Translations*, new ed. (London, 1954), 99.

The Martyrdom of Saints Cosmas and Damian. Panel from the predella of
the San Marco altarpiece.

IV

MARTYRDOM AND THE MUSE

The San Marco altarpiece manifests the mystery of martyrdom. After the Virgin and Child, its chief figures are saints who washed their robes in the blood of the Lamb. At the centre are St Cosmas and St Damian, who suffered in the persecution of Diocletian; they were the De Medicis' patrons, and their lives and deaths were portrayed in the side panels of the predella.

In the main altarpiece, on the left stands St Lawrence, one of the seven deacons of the Roman Church, martyred with Pope Sixtus II in 258 under the Emperor Valerian. He is one of the most honoured martyrs of the Church. As St Augustine reminds us, Lawrence is a kind of primatial martyr because he is deacon of a primatial Church: 'Just as Rome cannot be hidden, so Lawrence's crown cannot be hidden.'[1] On the right is St Peter Martyr, Peter of Verona, protomartyr of the Dominicans, killed by a hatchet blow in 1252. As he died, he dipped his finger in his blood and wrote the words *Credo in Deum*. Fra Angelico shows him as he will be seen in his risen body on the last day, with the wound in his head as an eternal badge of beauty. There is an important link between these four martyrs: they are all friends of the poor. According to St Ambrose and St Augustine, when Lawrence was asked by the tribunal for the treasure of the

[1] *Sermo 303*, 1; PL 38, 1393. Angelico painted a glorious sequence on St Lawrence's life for the chapel of Pope Nicholas V.

Church, he brought forth the starving and homeless.[2] Cosmas and Damian were 'unmercenary physicians', who served the poor without fee. As we hear in *The Golden Legend*, written by the thirteenth-century Dominican Jacobus de Voragine: 'They were learned in the art of medicine, and of leechcraft, and received so great grace of God that they healed all maladies and languors, not only of men but also cured and healed beasts. And did all for the love of God without taking of any reward.'[3] And Peter Martyr was a mendicant, vowed to Lady Poverty. His only gold was the Good News he preached to the poor: *Credo in Deum.*

In this final chapter, I should like to speak about the beautiful holiness of martyrdom and the holy beauty in art that it has begotten. The blood of the martyrs is the seed of the Church. Wherever it has been scattered, her mission has flowered and borne fruit. 'Going, they went and wept, casting their seeds. But coming, they shall come with joyfulness, carrying their sheaves' (Ps 125:6f.). One of the most abundant of these tear-sown sheaves has been sacred art. Since earliest times, from the Catacombs in fact, the martyrs have been the fertile source of sacred beauty in the Church. Like most of the great iconographers of the Tradition, Blessed Angelico delighted in glorifying the 'aeterni Christi munera, et martyrum victorias', the eternal gifts of Christ and the victories of His martyrs. The blood of the martyrs is the seed of the Church's art.

[2] St Ambrose, *De officiis ministrorum* 2, 28, 40; PL 16, 149BC; St Augustine, *Sermo 302*, 9, 8; PL 38, 1388–89. Of the poor, St Ambrose says: 'What better treasures does Christ have than those in whom He said He dwells, "For I was hungry, and you gave me to eat . . ."?' (*De officiis ministrorum* 2, 28, 40).

[3] Jacobus de Voragine, *The Golden Legend, or Lives of the Saints as Englished by William Caxton*, vol. 5 (London, 1900), 173.

1. The Art of Martyrdom

The Artist-Martyr

Some of the Church's martyrs were artists. One martyr, St Cecilia, is the Christian muse of a whole art. When the Academy of Music was founded in Rome in 1584, it was placed under her patronage. In seventeenth- and eighteenth-century England there were annual music festivals on St Cecilia's feast day, for which Purcell and Handel wrote some of their most splendid music. In the Paris of the last century, Solemn Mass was sung on St Cecilia's Day in the church of St Eustache, with the Conservatory orchestra accompanying a Mass setting specially composed for the occasion. The nineteenth-century movement for the restoration of the Church's sacred music also placed itself under St Cecilia's heavenly protection.[4]

How the martyr of the second or third century came to preside over so much of the music of the second millennium is a mystery. Till recently, the conventional scholarly wisdom has been that it is based on a medieval misunderstanding. In the late fifth-century account of her martyrdom, we are told that, at her wedding, while the organ played, Cecilia 'sang in her heart to God alone'. When this passage was sung as an antiphon at Lauds and Vespers, it was shortened; the words 'in her heart' (*in corde suo*) were omitted, suggesting that Cecilia sang out loud to the accompaniment of a musical instrument.[5] This scene was then represented in countless paintings, most beautifully of all in Raphael's *Ecstasy of Saint Cecilia*.

In 1994, Thomas Connolly, Professor of Music at the University of Pennsylvania, offered a new interpretation. He argued

[4] See the articles on 'Cecilia' and 'Cecilian Festivals' in *The New Grove Dictionary of Music and Musicians*, ed. S. Sadie, vol. 4 (London, 1980), 45–47.

[5] See H. Quentin, 'Sainte Cécile', *Dictionnaire d'archéologie chrétienne et de liturgie*, vol. 2/2, 2721f.

that St Cecilia's connection with music is more ancient and with deeper roots in theology than has hitherto been suspected. His starting point is the Raphael *Ecstasy*, in which Cecilia, in the company of St Paul, St John, St Mary Magdalen, and St Augustine, gazes up to Heaven, with an organ apparently slipping from her hand, while a viol, a tambourine, and other instruments lie scattered at her feet. The painting illustrates a text from Job: 'My harp is turned into mourning, my organ into the voice of those who weep' (Job 30:31). Raphael provides Connolly with the key that unlocks the mystery of Cecilia. The saints in this picture are people in whom God's grace accomplished a sudden and dramatic change of direction in their lives. In the life of Cecilia, there is a twofold change, not only from bloody agony to heavenly bliss, but from the merriment of an earthly wedding to the joy of her virginal nuptials with Christ. Cecilia on her wedding night reveals to her husband Valerian that she is vowed to virginity. He is baptized and finally, like his wife and with his brother, dies for Christ. Connolly argues that music is rightly connected with Cecilia not only because it can accomplish natural changes of emotion in our souls but because, in the Church's Tradition, it symbolizes the supernatural changes accomplished by the grace of the Holy Spirit.

> Change—deep change, in the spiritual order—is the constant in the veneration of Cecilia, the single theme on which most of the cult terms encountered in this study are but variations. Light from darkness, clarity out of confusion, mutation, *motus*, working, *impetus*, busyness, *operatio*—all are manifestations of the love that moves the sun and stars, and whose influence, transmitted in the works of grace, turns mourning into joy.[6]

The Bridegroom transfigures Cecilia's life into a work of art of singular beauty. According to St Albert, her heavenly 'aureole' has all the colours of the palette of grace:

[6] T. Connolly, *Mourning into Joy: Music, Raphael, and Saint Cecilia* (New Haven, 1994), 260.

Blessed Cecilia carries off the aureole, a garland woven from three kinds of flowers—the lily, the rose, and the violet. She carries off the lily, because she was a pure virgin. She bears the rose, because she suffered for Christ. She also wears the violet, because she converted to the Lord the two brothers, Tiburtius and Valerian, and many others. Thus it is written that, while Blessed Cecilia still lived on earth, the Angel of the Lord brought her a crown from Heaven, most delicately prepared from fragrant flowers.[7]

Jesuit Martyr-Poets

St Edmund Campion, Jesuit martyr, might have been one of Elizabethan England's greatest men of letters, the equal of Sidney and Spenser; but instead he took the path to Rome—and to Tyburn. In 1566 he was elected by the University of Oxford to welcome the Queen on her visitation. He was twenty-six and had been a Fellow of St John's for nine years. He had attracted around him, as Evelyn Waugh says in his biography, 'a group of pupils over whom he exerted an effortless and comprehensive influence; they crowded to his lectures, imitated his habits of speech, his mannerisms, and his clothes, and were proud to style themselves "Campionists".'[8] Campion had a similar effect on Elizabeth. He dazzled her with the elegance of his Latinity and the courtesy of his compliments. Before the court left Oxford, Cecil and Leicester had promised him their patronage.

Another young don, Tobie Matthew, also attracted the Queen's attention. He enjoyed the career that Campion never knew. Every glory of Anglican Church and state was heaped upon him: President of St John's, Dean of Christ Church, Vice-Chancellor, Dean and Bishop of Durham, Archbishop of York.

[7] *Sermo 49 de Beata Caecilia*; *Beati Alberti Magni opera omnia*, ed. A. Borgnet, vol. 13 (Paris, 1891), 605.

[8] *Edmund Campion*, 2d ed. (London, 1947), 8.

He married admirably [Waugh tells us] a widow of stout Protestant principles and unique place in the new clerical caste . . . Frances Barlow, widow of Matthew Parker, Junior; she was notable in her generation as having a bishop for her father, an archbishop for her father-in-law, an archbishop for her husband, and four bishops for her brothers. Tobie Matthew died full of honours in 1628. There, but for the Grace of God, went Edmund Campion.[9]

In 1571 Campion was received into the Catholic Church at Douai, and ten years later he was martyred for his faith and his priesthood—racked, then hanged, drawn, and quartered. This son of St Ignatius had made a complete surrender of himself to the Lord Jesus and His Bride: all his freedom, the whole of his memory, understanding, and will. God's grace and the love of Him were wealth—and beauty—enough; with such treasures, he asked for nothing more. In the *Rationes decem*, writing from his poverty and danger, he made this appeal to the dons of the universities in their comfort and ease:

Gold, glory, pleasures, lusts. Despise them. What are they but bowels of earth, high-sounding air, a banquet of worms, fair dunghills. Scorn them. Christ is rich, who will maintain you. He is a King, who will provide you. He is a sumptuous entertainer, who will feast you. *He is beautiful, who will give in abundance all that can make you happy.* Enrol yourselves in His service, that with Him you may gain triumphs, and show yourselves men truly most learned, truly most illustrious.[10]

Like Cecilia, Campion left the choir of the world for the Catholic consort of Christ. And yet, though his golden tongue was stilled, he sang from Heaven. Through his example and prayers, God poured out abundant new riches of sanctity and

[9] Ibid., 17.

[10] St Edmund Campion, *Ten Reasons Proposed to His Adversaries for Disputation in the Name of the Faith and Presented to the Illustrious Members of Our Universities*, new ed. (London, 1914), 145. The first edition of the Latin original was printed, to the peril of all concerned, at Stonor in 1581.

art, the beauty of holiness and the holiness of beauty, upon the hunted Catholics of England.

The execution of St Edmund Campion on December 1, 1581, was a turning point in the persecution of the Catholic Church in England. 'By it the Government finally committed themselves to the plan of fierce repression of the old religion culminating in the ferocious penal act of 1585.'[11] It had exactly the opposite effect to the one intended by the Queen's ministers. The steadfastness of Campion and his companions inspired many Catholics to a new fervour and, in the case of Henry Walpole, to offer himself to the Jesuits for priesthood on the English mission. He himself was executed at York on April 7, 1595. Campion's martyrdom also inspired Walpole to write the poem 'Why Do I Use My Paper, Ink, and Pen', in which he shows how Campion, by dying for the true faith, has attained a higher eloquence, the noblest rhetoric of all.

> England, look up, thy soil is stained with blood,
> thou hast made martyrs many of thine own,
> if thou hast grace their deaths will do thee good,
> the seed will take which in such blood is sown,
> and Campion's learning fertile so before,
> thus watered too, must needs of force be more.
>
> You thought perhaps, when learned Campion dies,
> his pen must cease, his sugared tongue be still,
> but you forgot how his death it cries,
> how far beyond the sound of tongue and quill,
> you did not know how rare and great a good
> it was to write his precious gifts in blood.
>
> His hurdle draws us with him to the cross,
> his speeches there provoke us for to die,

[11] L. I. Guiney, *Recusant Poets, with a Selection of Their Work*, vol. 1, *Saint Thomas More to Ben Jonson* (London and New York, 1938), 175.

his death doth say this life is but a loss,
his martyred blood from Heaven to us doth cry,
his first and last, and all conspire in this,
to show the way that leadeth unto bliss.[12]

One of Walpole's confrères, a brother both in the Society and in martyrdom, was to become one of the greatest poets of the Elizabethan age. While, for Campion, the priesthood meant the sacrifice of literature, for St Robert Southwell, the nine years of his priestly mission in England (concluding with his arrest in June 1592) inspired him to write his English verse. In a preface written to his cousin, Southwell finds the model and source of Christian poetry in the Word made flesh Himself.

> Christ Himself, by making a hymn the conclusion of His Last Supper and the Prologue to the first Pageant of His Passion, gave His Spouse a method to imitate, as in the office of the Church it appeareth, and all men a pattern to know the true use of this measured and footed style.[13]

Christ is the heart of this poetry—the incarnate Word in His mysteries, especially the mysteries of His infancy:

Let folly praise that fancy loves, I praise and love that
    Child,
Whose heart, no thought, whose tongue, no word,
    whose hand no deed defiled.
I praise Him most, I love Him best, all praise and love
    is His:
While Him I love, in Him I live, and cannot live amiss.[14]

Southwell dwells, too, on the Agony in the Garden and 'Sin's heavy load' that so hard-pressed the Saviour. It is my sin, he says, that bruises these shoulders and wounds this Heart.

[12] Ibid., 178f.
[13] *The Poems of Robert Southwell, S.J.*, ed. J. H. McDonald and N. P. Brown (Oxford, 1967), 1.
[14] 'A Child My Choice', in ibid., 13.

O Lord, my sin doth over-charge thy breast,
The poise thereof doth force thy knees to bow;
Yea flat thou fallest with my faults oppressed,
And bloody sweat runs trickling from thy brow.
But had they not to earth thus pressed thee,
Much more they would in Hell have pestered me.[15]

He bids the sinner to turn back to the pierced Heart, to enter the open side: 'O royal rift, O worthy wound, Come harbour me a weary guest.'[16] He weeps in the person of the penitent Peter[17] and the blushing Magdalen.[18] He repeats the '*Peccavi*' of King David. Sin's load is crushing, but by God's mercy it is out-weighed, when there is contrition, confession, and satisfaction. Remember that the Church built on Peter has the power of the keys, the Sacrament of Christ's forgiveness. Southwell offers a consolation and a challenge to the fallen-away Catholics of England. It is not too late. Look up to Heaven, to the beauty of Christ in His saints. 'Seek flowers of Heaven. . . . Graze not on worldly withered weed.'[19]

Like Campion's, Southwell's noblest lines were written in his life's blood. Seeing his courage and the sweet calm of his hope in the Crucified Christ, the Tyburn crowd pleaded with the hang-man to let him die on the gallows rather than be drawn while still breathing. Lord Mountjoy, the future conqueror of Ireland, cried out in high grief: 'I cannot answer for his religion, but I wish to God that my soul may be with his.'[20]

---

[15] Ibid., 17.
[16] 'Man to the Wound in Christ's Side', in ibid., 72.
[17] 'St Peter's Complaint' in its various versions, in ibid., 29ff., 75ff.
[18] 'Mary Magdalene's Blush', in ibid., 32.
[19] 'Seek Flowers of Heaven', in ibid., 52.
[20] C. Devlin, *The Life of Robert Southwell: Poet and Martyr* (London, 1956), 324.

Martyrdom and Music for the Mass

The death of Campion transformed both the life and the art of William Byrd, the *Brittanicae Musicae Parens*, the 'Father of British Music'.[21] The 'holiness of beauty' in his later music is linked, not merely extrinsically and accidentally, but intrinsically and essentially with the 'beauty of holiness' in the lives of the English martyrs. In 1581, the year of Campion's martyrdom, Byrd was approaching forty. Although he was a Catholic, he had been employed for most of his professional life by the Anglican establishment, first as organist and choirmaster of Lincoln Cathedral and since 1570 as Gentleman of the Chapel Royal.

The first sign of Byrd's reinvigorated Catholicism is his music for Walpole's lament for the brave young Jesuits, 'with its emphatic setting of the phrase, "Their glorious death" '.[22] His wife had already been cited for recusancy in 1577. His two surviving letters, dating from 1581, are petitions for assistance for a Catholic family in need as a result of persecution.

In 1583, at Hurleyford, a mansion set amidst great woods in the Chilterns, the home of the Catholic Bold family, Byrd met two of the Jesuit missionaries who were later to die for the faith, St Henry Garnet and St Robert Southwell. Southwell, as we know, was a great poet, while Garnet was an enthusiastic amateur musician. The house party was a tonic for all: for the priests, peace for mind and body after the terrors of the high road, and for Byrd, spiritual refreshment through the Sacraments and the fellowship of zealous priests. A contemporary account says:

> We were very happy, and our friends made it apparent how pleased they were to have us. . . . During those days it was just as if we were celebrating an uninterrupted octave of some great

[21] I have been much helped by J. Kerman's article on Byrd in *New Grove Dictionary* 3:537–52.

[22] David Wulstan, 'Birdus tantum natus decorare magistrum', in *Byrd Studies*, ed. A. Brown and R. Turbet (Cambridge, 1992), 121.

feast. Mr Byrd, the very famous English musician and organist, was among the company. Earlier he had been attached to the Queen's Chapel where he had great reputation. *But he had sacrificed everything for the faith.*[23]

Father Christopher Devlin describes the meeting of Byrd and Southwell as follows:

> The beauty of Church music was one of the chief means by which the recusants kept up their spirits. Between Southwell and Byrd there is no record of any further meeting; but it is natural to suppose that there were many. Byrd was engaged at this time in setting to music the poems contained in his *Psalms, Sonnets, and Songs of Sadness and Piety*, which did more than anything to preserve the medieval lyric in English poetry; and it was probably with his help that Southwell first became acquainted with contemporary English verse in its current manuscript form.[24]

Byrd did not lose his position in the Queen's Chapel, but there is no doubt that, henceforth, he was in danger of his life. His house in Harlington was twice searched, and he was repeatedly battered with fines for recusancy. His powerful patrons, including the Queen herself, usually came to his rescue, but support from such persons was anything but reliable. The thought of destitution and violent death never left his mind. In an official document of 1605, the Byrds are branded as 'seducers' in the Catholic cause.

In a new spirit of Catholic loyalty, Byrd began to develop the Latin motet. The texts may have been chosen to give comfort to the hounded Catholic flock. *Circumspice, Hierusalem* (cf. Bar 4:36) sings of the exiled children of Jerusalem, coming from the East, rejoicing for the honour of God, while in *Deus, venerunt gentes* (cf. Ps 78:1), the heathens defile the Temple, and the flesh of the saints becomes meat for the beasts of the earth.[25] In both

[23] Devlin, *Life*, 114f.
[24] Ibid., 115.
[25] Cf. Kerman, *New Grove Dictionary* 3:541.

motets, we cannot fail to hear echoes of Campion, Garnet, Southwell, and the rest, arriving from France with youthful ardour and dying hideous deaths for the Mass, the priesthood, the papacy, and the truth of Christ's Church.

In 1593 the Byrds moved farther away from London, to a part of Essex where the Catholic Petre family had influence. William attended the Masses celebrated secretly at the Petres' house, Ingatestone Hall, and it was doubtless for them that he composed some, if not all, of the pieces in his *Gradualia*, which is the largest collection of his music that he ever made. His glorious Masses—for three, four, and five voices—were also probably written for the Petre family. The surviving copies of them are bound with copies of the *Gradualia*: the Masses cover the Ordinary, the *Gradualia* cover the Propers.[26] Byrd was now the liturgical composer of a martyred Church.

Although there are pre-Reformation English influences on Byrd's Masses, they are written in the style and spirit of Tridentine Catholicism. He wanted to think with the Church, the Church that at Trent had laid down new norms for sacred music. For example, unlike the earlier English Masses, they contain a setting of the *Kyrie*, whereas, in the old Sarum Rite, the *Kyrie* was 'troped', that is to say, the invocations '*Kyrie eleison*' and '*Christe eleison*' were decked out with interpolated petitions, which had their own music.[27] Like Victoria, and again in the spirit of the Tridentine reform, Byrd strives to make the text as clear as possible: the music is for the Word, not the Word for the music. In the preface to the first part of the *Gradualia*, he explains how close study of the text of the Roman liturgy moved him to find the right notes for the setting. In other words, the music is the fruit of meditation, of *lectio divina* of the Scriptures and the liturgical books. In the four-part Mass, for example, he

---

[26] Cf. J. Caldwell, *The Oxford History of English Music*, vol. 1, *From the Beginnings to c. 1715* (Oxford, 1991), 384.

[27] Ibid., 385.

gives solemn stress to the words *unam, sanctam, catholicam et apostolicam ecclesiam* in the Creed, and in the supplication at the end of the *Ave Verum Corpus*, he begs for mercy from Jesus in the Host: 'O dulcis, O pie, O Jesu, Fili Mariae, miserere mei', O sweet, O loving, O Jesu, Son of Mary, have mercy on me.

Dialogues of the Carmelites

The martyrdom of the Carmelite nuns of Compiègne during the French Revolution has inspired four great works of twentieth-century art—four works, four art forms: a novel, a film, a play, an opera. First, Gertrud von Le Fort writes a novel. Then Georges Bernanos prepares the screenplay for a movie based on the novel. Albert Béguin produces it on the stage. Finally, Francis Poulenc takes up the screenplay as a libretto for his *Dialogues des Carmélites*, one of the greatest operas of the twentieth century.

Bernanos plunges into the theological depths of the drama. As the clouds of death gather (Bernanos wrote it in 1948 when he himself was dying of cancer), many of the nuns are bravely ready, but Sister Blanche of the Agony of Christ cannot master her fear of death. Her sisters—out of love, by prayer—take that fear from her and upon themselves. The old Prioress dies a strange and disturbing death, one that does not seem to fit her. The Sub-Prioress, Marie de l'Incarnation, urges the community to take an oath of martyrdom, and yet she does not die with the others; her cross is to go on living. As for Blanche herself, in the end she dies for Christ without dread. These acts of 'substitution and exchange' are not performed by the sisters' unaided human powers, but only through, with, and in Christ, in whose 'adorable Heart' in Gethsemane 'all human anguish was divinized.' [28] There is no hybris in the martyrs. However poor they may be,

---

[28] Bernanos makes one of his characters say: 'When we consider these things from the Garden of Gethsemane, where all human anguish was divinized in the Adorable Heart of Our Lord, the distinction between fear and

they know that their Lord and Master was infinitely poorer. They imitate Him humbly, at a distance. It is by His grace that in them the *Communio Sanctorum* becomes a living and dramatic reality. In the dying words of another Bernanos character, 'all is grace'.

Culture and Counterculture

The martyrs obey the Apostle when he says: 'Do not be conformed to this world, but be transformed by the renewal of your mind, that you may prove what is the will of God, what is good and acceptable and perfect' (Rom 12:2). There is nothing negative about this resistance to the present age, this *contemptus mundi*. On the contrary, it is a condition of the martyrs' positive love. The believer cannot cooperate with the Son's mission of saving the world unless he cooperates with the Spirit's mission of convincing the world of its sin. Since, as St Augustine says, the world lives by *cupiditas*, conformity to the world is bound to destroy *caritas*. The martyrs demonstrate that what nowadays is called 'inculturation', the transformation of a culture by the gospel, can take place only through purgation of the culture's defilement and the illumination of its darkness.

Christopher Dawson once showed how, during the Middle Ages, what he called the 'dualism of Church and world' was 'the principal source of that dynamic element which is of such decisive significance for Western culture'.[29] It was precisely during what now we would call the 'Christian centuries' that the faithful were most sharply conscious of the Pauline challenge to be unconformed to the world. To us the twelfth century seems a golden age of Christian culture, but to the men of the time it

---

courage seems to me not far from superfluous . . .' (*Dialogues des Carmélites* [Paris, 1949], 111).

[29] Christopher Dawson, *Religion and the Rise of Western Culture*, new ed. (New York, 1958), 68.

was 'dark with the threat of the coming doom'.[30] Its outlook is typified by Bernard of Morlais's poem: 'Hora novissima, tempora sunt, vigilemus . . .', The world is very evil, the times are waxing late; Be sober and keep vigil, the Judge is at the gate. Cultures are transformed by the unworldly, by those who bring them, at whatever the cost, the salt, light, and leaven of God's Word. The blood of the martyrs is indeed the seed of the Church. Through their wounds, Christian faith and charity are poured out anew to water the wasteland of the world.

The Spiritual Beauty of the Martyrs

After the Mother of God and the Apostles, the Church's martyrs have the greatest spiritual beauty among the saints. They are refulgent through the Blood of the Lamb. Their death is like a jewel, 'precious in the eyes of the Lord'. 'Confessio et pulchritudo in conspectu eius', sang the Dominicans of San Marco on the feast of St Lawrence: 'Honour and beauty are His escort; worship and magnificence the attendants of His shrine' (cf. Ps 95:6). There is no Christian cult of death, and there cannot be. When St Ambrose writes 'On the Good of Death', he means death transfigured by the crucified and risen Jesus. 'God did not make death,' says the Wise Man, 'and He does not delight in the death of the living' (Wis 1:13). Though the material body is mortal by nature, God did not want mankind to suffer the separation of soul from body. According to St Thomas, since man is by nature a unity of body and soul, the rending of the union in death is *contra naturam*.[31] God, therefore, endowed Adam and Eve with a wonderful preternatural gift giving them the possibility of escaping bodily death. By their sin, they lost that gift for themselves and for us, their children. Thus 'sin came into the world through one man, and through sin death' (Rom 5:12).

[30] Ibid., 204.
[31] Cf. *Summa contra gentiles* 4, 79.

Death is no friend of man. It is the last enemy to be destroyed (cf. 1 Cor 15:26), a monster to be crushed. It is trampled upon by the incarnate Son of God in His Death on the Cross and His Resurrection from the tomb. The Lord Jesus has driven a way, a passage, through death: dying with Him and in Him, by the grace of the Holy Spirit, we can reach the house and heart of the Father. It is not, then, death that the martyrs seek: it is Christ. St Paul longs to depart and to be with the Lord (cf. Phil 1:23). 'Him I seek who died for us', cries Ignatius of Antioch, 'Him I desire who rose again for us!'[32] In the living waters of the Spirit, he hears the whisper of the Son: 'Come to the Father!'[33] And so he begs his brethren: 'Leave me to imitate the Passion of my God.'[34]

St Thomas Aquinas says that the endurance of death is praise-worthy, not in itself, but when directed towards some good ac-tion of faith or love of God.[35] The beauty of martyrdom is the beauty of the martyr's heroic virtue, of the Theological Virtues of faith, hope, and charity exalted to a valiant degree. 'Martyr' means 'witness', and so, in the first place, the martyr is a 'witness of the Christian faith'.[36] He is faith-ful, full of faith, even unto a most terrible death. Thus he shows forth the splendour of truth. As St Augustine says, 'they were true witnesses because they spoke the truth, and by speaking the truth, they received their crowns.[37] The martyr manifests the loveliness of objective truth and exposes the shamefulness of relativism. There is nothing in Liberalism or Modernism for the world to persecute, for the liberal's whole programme is to worship the world's every whim. By contrast, the Christian martyr, 'standing firm in truth

---

[32] *Epistola ad Romanos* 6; in J. B. Lightfoot, ed., *The Apostolic Fathers*, pt. 2, vol. 2, sec. 1 (London, 1885), 218.

[33] Ibid., no. 7; 224.

[34] Ibid., no. 6; 220.

[35] Cf. ST 2a2ae 124, 3.

[36] Ibid., 124, 4.

[37] *Sermo 328*, 2; PL 38, 1452.

and justice against the attack of his persecutors',[38] lets truth be seen and admired in all its glory. His witness is a theological aesthetic.

According to St Ignatius of Antioch, the martyrdom of the Apostles was a confession of faith in the truth of the bodily Resurrection of Our Lord.

> As for me, I know and I believe Him to be in the flesh, even after the Resurrection. When He came to Peter and his companions, He said to them, 'Lay hold and handle me, and see that I am no bodiless demon.' And straightway they touched Him and believed, having contact with His actual flesh and blood. This was how they came by their contempt for death; this was how they mastered death. After His Resurrection, He also ate and drank with them in the flesh, though united with the Father in the Spirit.[39]

The faith of the martyrs is vivified by perfect charity. St Thomas says that charity is the primary motivating power behind martyrdom, the virtue that 'commands' it, while the virtue that elicits it, that sustains it, is fortitude; martyrdom is the noblest proof of the perfection of charity.[40] The martyr does not die in grim attachment to an idea but in grateful love for a person, the Divine Person of the incarnate Son of God, who 'loved me and gave Himself up for me' (cf. Gal 2:20). In Balthasar's words, the martyr dies in 'a passion of responsive love'.[41] With Ignatius of Antioch, the white-robed army all cry out: 'Leave me to imitate the passion of my God!'[42]

Martyrdom by blood is a gift given to the few, and yet every Christian must be ready to confess Christ crucified in the face

---

[38] ST 2a2ae 124, 1.

[39] *Epistola ad Smyrnaeos* 3; in Lightfoot, *Apostolic Fathers*, pt. 2, vol. 2, sec. 1, 294f.

[40] ST 2a2ae 124, 3.

[41] Hans Urs von Balthasar, *New Elucidations* (San Francisco, 1986), 288.

[42] *Epistola ad Romanos* 6; in Lightfoot, *Apostolic Fathers*, pt. 2, vol. 2, sec. 1, 220.

of a hostile world. Not only those who share the apostolic min-istry but all the baptized are sent out 'as sheep in the midst of wolves' (Mt 20:16). The world will hate the disciple as it hated the Master; it will attack anyone in whom it can see a likeness of Christ. We may, therefore, conclude with Balthasar:

> [P]ersecution constitutes the normal condition of the Church in her relation to the world, and martyrdom is the normal con-dition of the professed Christian. This does not mean that the Church will necessarily be persecuted at all times and in all places, but if it does happen at certain times and in certain places, then it should be remembered that this is a sign of that special grace promised to her: 'But I have said these things to you, that when their hour comes you may remember that I told you of them' (Jn 16:4).[43]

It is precisely for their witness to Christ in the face of the world that those incorporated into Christ in Baptism are strengthened by the Holy Spirit in Confirmation. We are called to live and die in the truth of our baptismal identity as sons-in-the-Son. The eternal Son-made-man wants us, by the grace of the Holy Spirit, to share in His 'Passover' to the Father, first in Baptism and then in our actual living and dying. Again to quote Balthasar, 'God does not content himself with our heartfelt thanks. He wants to be able to recognize his own Son in Christian men and women.'[44] The Father calls all Christians, and moves them in the Holy Spirit, to die witnessing to Christ, in friendship with Him through faith and charity. Thus, as the poet Charles Péguy saw, because of the intimate union of the Head with His members, even 'the least of the sick' can die a martyr's death, a witnessing death of grateful love for Jesus.[45] Such a death bears beautiful fruit for the whole Mystical Body.

---

[43] *The Moment of Christian Witness* (San Francisco, 1994), 21–22.

[44] Ibid., 25.

[45] 'The Crowned Head and the least of His members are united by a bond so perfect that the least of the sick, in his bed, is allowed to imitate the suffer-ing of Jesus on the Cross. The least of the sick, in his bed, literally imitates,

According to the constant teaching of the Catholic Church, martyrdom, Baptism of Blood, is an efficacious substitute for Baptism of Water. It confers the Grace of Justification and remits not only all sin, Original and personal, but also all punishment for sin.[46] The martyr-poet St Robert Southwell, in his *Epistle of Comfort*, quotes St Cyprian and St Augustine and argues that martyrdom thus confers on the soul a wondrous spiritual beauty: '[A]s no offence committed before Baptism can do the baptized any harm, so also doth martyrdom so cleanse the soul from all spot of former corruption that it giveth thereunto a most undefiled beauty.'[47] It has this advantage over Baptism of Water: it sets the martyr free at once from concupiscence and the struggles of this life and gives him immediate entry into Heaven.

> And if St Chrysostom, extolling Baptism saith that it not only maketh us free but also holy; not only holy but just; not only just but children; not only children but heirs; not only heirs with Christ but members of Christ; not only members but temples; not only temples but also instruments of the Holy Ghost; then may I further enlarge myself in the praise of martyrdoms and say that martyrdom giveth a freedom void of all servitude, a holiness and justice without any fault or fear of loss. It so maketh us children, that we cannot become enemies. It maketh us heirs with Christ, not only of His grace but also of His glory. It maketh us members that cannot be cut off, temples that cannot be defiled, such instruments of the Holy Ghost as cannot be abused. Finally, it giveth us the crown,

---

effectively imitates, efficaciously imitates, the very Passion of Jesus, the martyrdom of Jesus and of other saints and martyrs. . . . [T]he least of the sick can, by a kind of appropriation, a consecration towards God, turn his illness into martyrdom, make his malady the matter of martyrdom' ('Un nouveau théologien, M. Fernand Laudet', Deuxième cahier de la treizième série, September 24, 1911; in Charles Péguy, *Oeuvres en prose 1909–1914* [Paris, 1957], 858f.).

[46] Cf. ST 3a 68, 2, ad 2.

[47] St Robert Southwell, *An Epistle of Comfort*, new ed. (London, 1966), 163.

whereof Baptism is the pledge; in all which points it is superior unto it.[48]

The martyr shares in the Paschal paradox of the theological aesthetic: his hour of highest spiritual beauty is a moment of utmost bodily degradation. As Fra Angelico sang with his brethren on the feast of St Cosmas and St Damian, 'they have thrown the corpses of thy servants, Lord, to feed the birds of Heaven; wild beasts prey on the carrion of the just' (Ps 78:2). Southwell explains the mystery by an analogy:

> Personable men of comely feature, though they be by sickness or dirt disfigured, yet keep they the tokens of seemliness; yea and then their seemliness is most seen, when it is compared with some contrary deformity. And so it is in God's martyrs: even in the depth of worldly disgrace do they show the glorious grace and beauty of their mind, and when their virtue encountereth with the persecutor's vice, then doth it shine brightest, and is unto the beholders most pleasing and amiable.[49]

It is by the grace that the incarnate Son merited for them on the Cross that the martyrs take up their cross and follow Him. Why, asks St Augustine, is the death of His holy ones so 'precious in the sight of the Lord'? Because it was His most precious Blood that paid the price for them.[50] Our Lord does more than merely offer the martyrs an example, walking on the road ahead of them. He is the One who carves it out, driving a royal highway through death's trackless waste. He is Himself the Way, the One through and with and in whom we pass over to the Father. For us, as our Head, in Gethsemane, the incarnate Son took the fear of death upon Himself, and now, says St Augustine, He speaks to us:

> Recognize yourself in me, so that you need not despair when you are troubled but can turn your gaze back to your Head and

---

[48] Ibid., 166.
[49] Ibid., 180.
[50] *Sermo 328*, 1; PL 38, 1452.

say to yourself, 'When the Lord said, "My soul is troubled", we were in Him, we were being signified. We are troubled, but not lost.'[51]

Only through the sacrificed flesh and blood of Christ in the Eucharist is a man made capable of martyrdom. As Balthasar says:

> I blossom on the grave of the God who died for me. I sink my roots deep into the nourishing soil of His flesh and blood. The love which I draw in faith from this soil can be of no other kind than the love of one who is buried.[52]

United to the God-Man, we are like one mystical person, and so through His Sacrifice on the Cross, re-presented by the Church in the Holy Sacrifice of the Mass, our suffering can be transfigured.

Laughing Martyrdom

We must not be too intense. Christian martyrdom is not tragedy. Our spiritual battle against the world, the flesh, and the Devil will continue until our last breath, but we fight in the strength of the risen Christ, the conqueror of Hades, the overcomer of the world. That is why, as Our Lady says in Chesterton's poem 'The Ballad of the White Horse', 'the men signed of the sign of Christ/ Go gaily in the dark.'[53] Even the falling into dust of our bodies cannot shake us, because in the very Body He took from the Virgin the divine Word has risen from the tomb, trampling upon death, and through that glorious Body, with which He feeds us at the altar, He will raise up our bodies on the last day.

The Easter Mystery places the 'Theo-drama' of salvation beyond the opposition of tragedy and comedy. Here is a catastrophe

---

[51] *Sermo 305*, 4; PL 38, 1399.

[52] Balthasar, *New Elucidations*, 13.

[53] G. K. Chesterton, *Collected Works*, vol. 10: *Collected Poetry*, pt. 1 (San Francisco, 1994), 216.

beyond all disasters, and yet this is a triumph surpassing all happy endings. According to Balthasar, in antiquity it was Greek tragedy rather than philosophy that was the great 'cipher' of Christ, but in Christianity, now that the Only-begotten of the Father has tasted and conquered death in the flesh, there can be no place for a tragedy of 'absolute gravity'.[54] Tragedy cannot be the dominant note in Christian literature. As Balthasar says in *Herrlichkeit*:

> It is no accident that, in Christian literature, comedy on the whole outweighs tragedy. In Shakespeare the two are finely balanced, but in the English novel, right up to Chesterton, it is humour which increasingly has the upper hand. Molière has more penetration than Racine, Goldoni more weight than Alfieri. In Austria, with Mozart, Raimund, Nestroy, Hofmannsthal, Christian light triumphs over bogus German gravity. . . . I am talking about the light of humour, for irony presumes to take on the perspective of God, while the pharisaism of satire sits in judgment (accusingly or leniently) on the faults of one's neighbour. . . . By contrast, the Christian humorist knows about the mysterious relationship between the wisdom of grace and the folly of sin and the abyss between them, at once open and closed.[55]

With similar insight, Chesterton notes how often the great Christian martyrs have been blessed with the grace of gentle good humour, thus proving that theirs is a transformed tragedy, a little pain held within the great pain of the God-Man. He loved the fact that the missionary priest St John Kemble died smoking 'in spite of the fury with which faddists like James the First were to fulminate against tobacco'.[56] Above all, he revered and revelled in the memory of St Thomas More:

> Behind his public life, which was so grand a tragedy, there was a private life that was perpetual comedy. . . . Everybody knows,

---

[54] Balthasar, H 3/1/1, 94ff.; GL 4, 101ff.

[55] Balthasar, H 3/1/2, 504; GL 5, 153.

[56] Chesterton, *Chaucer*, 299. G. K. gets his dates wrong. St John Kemble died in 1679, long after the death of James the First in 1625.

of course, that the comedy and the tragedy met, as they meet in Shakespeare, on that last high wooden stage where his drama ended.[57]

Francis Thompson gives us perhaps the best account of all of the meeting of tragedy and comedy in the life of More. In his poem 'To the English Martyrs' he writes:

> To the keen *accolade* and holy
> Thou didst bend low a sprightly knee,
> And jest Death out of gravity
> As a too sad-visaged friend;
> So, jocund, passing to the end
> Of thy laughing martyrdom;
> And now from travel art gone home
> Where, since gain of thee was given,
> Surely there is more mirth in Heaven.[58]

2. The Martyrdom of Art

When Christian men are martyred, so is Christian art. Iconoclasm did not die with the triumph of Orthodoxy in 843. In post-Reformation England, the burning and breaking of holy beauty was the work not only of Cromwell's soldiery in the seventeenth century but of Anglicanism's founding fathers in the sixteenth. Indeed, as Margaret Aston has shown,[59] the iconoclasm of the English Reformers was more violent even than that of Zwingli and Calvin, who at least opposed the breaking of stained glass; but in the Injunctions of Edward VI in 1547, even imagery in windows was to be destroyed.

[57] Chesterton, *The Well and the Shallows* (New York, 1935), 242.

[58] 'To the English Martyrs' in *The Poems of Francis Thompson*, new ed. (London, 1913), 285.

[59] See Margaret Aston, *England's Iconoclasts*, vol. 1, *Laws against Images* (Oxford, 1988).

Also, That they shall take away, utterly extinct and destroy all
shrines, covering of shrines, all tables, candlesticks, trindles or
rolls of wax, pictures, paintings, and all other monuments of
feigned miracles, pilgrimages, idolatry, and superstition: so that
there remain no memory of the same in walls, glass-windows, or
elsewhere within their churches or houses. And they shall ex-
hort their parishioners to do the like within their several
houses.[60]

Mrs Aston comments: 'Obliteration . . . was the order of the day.'[61]

The dogmatic teaching of the Second Council of Nicaea on
the veneration of images was widely rejected by the Anglican
divines: 'That childish council of Nice the Second', as Jewel
called it. William Laud, not himself an iconoclast and attacked
by the Puritans for his popish idolatry, had nonetheless no sym-
pathy for the Iconodule Council: 'That gross Council of
Nice'.[62] In Durham the fanatical Calvinist Dean Whittingham
stripped the cathedral bare of most of its sacred art. He pulled
out the holy water stoups for use in his kitchen. St Cuthbert's
shrine was dismantled. He caused the image of St Cuthbert 'to
be defaced and broken all in pieces, to the intent that there
should be no memory nor token of that holy man'.[63] His corporal cloth, held up as a banner at the battle of Neville's Cross,
was burnt by Mrs Whittingham 'in the notable contempt and
disgrace of all ancient and godly relics'.[64] The relics of St Bede
were scattered to the winds. Our Lady's altar, and all the altars,
were tossed into the backyards of the College. The images of

[60] *Visitation Articles and Injunctions of the Period of the Reformation*, ed. W. H.
Frere and W. M. Kennedy (Alcuin Club, 1910), 2:119f.; cited in Aston,
England's Iconoclasts, 1:256.

[61] Aston, *England's Iconoclasts*, 1:257.

[62] Cited in ibid., 1:55.

[63] *Rites of Durham: Being a Description or Brief Declaration of All the Ancient
Monuments, Rites and Customs Belonging or Being within the Monastical Church of
Durham before the Suppression*, Surtees Society, no. 107 (1903), 68f.

[64] Ibid., 27.

the Neville Screen were ripped out. The window into Heaven
had been smashed. Christendom was no longer one common-
wealth in this world and the next. There was to be no prayer
for the poor souls, no invoking of the blessed. Nor, in the new
doctrine of Justification, could there be a beauty in holiness.
For Whittingham's master (and probable brother-in-law) John
Calvin, Sanctifying Grace does not inwardly renew and beautify the soul. The new Protestant Justification, whether Lu-
theran or Calvinist, is extrinsic, a forensic transaction, the
covering of the dung of depraved human nature with the snow
of Christ's merits.[65]

The war on holy beauty in the England of Edward and Elizabeth was total war. To quote Mrs Aston again:

> What started with monastic shrines and abused pilgrimage im-
> ages, progressed to pictures and statues of all kinds, to church
> windows, to the crucifix, even to the cross itself. From the re-
> moval of some images the issue became the annihilation of
> them all. Images generated passionate feelings, and iconoclastic
> arguments were always several steps ahead of official enact-
> ments.[66]

Some of the Reformers denounced even mental images, the
icons of the soul. For St Thomas, it is from the data of sense

[65] 'Therefore, we explain justification simply as the acceptance with which
God receives us into His favour as righteous men. And we say that it consists in
the remission of sins and the imputation of Christ's righteousness' (*The Institutes of the Christian Religion*, bk.3, chap. 11, no. 2; vol. 1 [Philadelphia, 1960],
727). 'Now God's image is the perfect excellence of human nature which
shone in Adam before his defection, but was subsequently so vitiated and almost blotted out that nothing remains after the ruin except what is confused,
mutilated, and disease-ridden' (ibid., bk. 1, chap. 15, no. 4; 1:190). For Calvin,
there is an intrinsic corruption in fallen human nature, a 'depravity of nature':
'If these are the hereditary endowments of the human race, it is futile to seek
anything good in our nature' (ibid., bk. 2, chap. 3, no. 2; 1:291). By contrast,
the Catholic Church of Christ holds that Adam was 'wounded in what is
natural, deprived of what was gratuitously given': our fallen human nature is
deprived, not depraved, and in that deprivation is its disorder and deformity.

[66] Aston, *England's Iconoclasts*, 1:342.

experience that we abstract our ideas, and we deploy them through a constant 'conversion to images'. But, for John Hooper, fallen human nature is so intrinsically depraved that a picture in the mind will inevitably deceive and seduce. Natural knowledge of God is impossible, for any mental image of the Deity will be an idol. If anything reveals the tendency of the Reformation towards Manichaeanism, the rejection in religion of everything sensible, it is this astonishing declaration of disgust in one of his early writings:

> The mind of man, when it is not illuminated with the Spirit of God, nor governed by the Scripture, it imagineth and feigneth God to be like unto the imagination and conceit of his mind, and not as the Scripture teacheth.[67]

This is also Calvin's doctrine:

> Man's mind, full as it is of pride and boldness, dares to imagine a god according to its own capacity; as it sluggishly plods, indeed is overwhelmed with the coarsest ignorance, it conceives an un-reality and an empty appearance as God. To these evils a new wickedness joins itself, that man tries to express in his work the sort of God he has inwardly conceived. Therefore the mind begets an idol; the hand gives it birth.[68]

Throughout the last two centuries, in attacking the Church's beautiful holiness, the ideologies of godlessness have attacked also her holy beauty. In Revolutionary France and Communist Russia, in Nazi Germany and Civil War Spain, sacrilege was wielded like a sword. The horrors of the last of these conflicts are not well known in the English-speaking world, so let me briefly describe them. From the summer of 1936 onwards, the broad alliance of the Left waged war against the Catholic Church. It has been called, and it truly was, a Catholic holo-

---

[67] Ibid., 1:436.
[68] *Institutes*, bk. 1, chap. 11, no. 8; 1:108.

caust.[69] Thousands of priests, religious, and lay people were murdered. Churches were burnt and blown up. Tabernacles were smashed, and the Sacred Hosts defiled. The tombs of dead religious were opened, and their bodies propped up on the pavement. Crucifixes and statues of the saints were shot as if they were living persons.[70] Catholics kept their kitchen madonnas at the risk of their lives.

But the iconoclasm of the twentieth century has not just been a weapon of godless ideologies; it has also been the upshot of disordered theologies. The attack on dogmatic truth and moral goodness has been reinforced, perhaps even spearheaded, by the assault on liturgical beauty. Throughout the Latin Church, the Philistines have seized the sanctuary. The stone altar of sacrifice has been supplanted by a wooden communion table. The priest no longer looks to the East, whither Christ ascended and whence He will come again, but stares at the people, like the chairman of the board. The saints have been pulled from their niches. Petitionary lights no longer flicker by their shrines. In exact imitation of the Iconoclasts, bare crosses stand without the sacred corpus. The Holy of Holies has been exiled—banished from the central gaze and adoration of the faithful. The church building, icon of the Empyrean, looks like a shabby

---

[69] See Fray Justo Perez de Urbel, *Catholic Martyrs of the Spanish Civil War 1936–1939* (Kansas City, 1993).

[70] 'One day in the month of November 1936, six armed militia from the *Columna del Rosal* entered the house of the elderly parish priest who lay in bed with fever. Three of them began to search the house; the other two [sic] spent hours alongside the bed tormenting him without pause. No doubt noticing his tranquil state, they picked up a *Santo Cristo* that he had nearby which had been a treasured possession since his youth. They began to stick their knives into the Crucifix saying that they would do the same to all the priests. The priest said to them: "Do what you like to me, but what has the *Santo Cristo* done to deserve this? I am a priest, and I believe in Christ, and I love Him' (ibid., 73). Cf. also the great postwar novel, the *War and Peace* of modern Spanish literature, José María Gironella's *Los cipreses creen en Dios* (Barcelona, 1953) (ET, *The Cypresses Believe in God* [New York, 1955]).

warehouse, while the rectory, shelter of the servants of the poor
Christ, has become a sumptuous palace. Gregorian chant, declared by an ecumenical council to be 'proper to the Roman
liturgy' and to have 'the first place in liturgical actions',[71] has
been replaced by ditties of doubtful orthodoxy. The Latin language, sign and instrument of the Western Church's unity and
of the purity of her doctrine, has all but disappeared from parish
worship, while vernacular texts, already ugly and inaccurate,
have become the plaything of Neo-Modernism and Eco-
feminism. The integrity and thus the beauty of the Roman rite
have almost been destroyed.

There is a terrible resemblance between the despoiling of sacred liturgy and the destruction of sacred life. In both cases,
innocence is the victim. The Lamb of God suffers afresh—in the
persons of His little ones and under the lowly appearances of
bread. When men lose the sense of the sacred, they lose the
sense of God, and when men lose the sense of God, they lose all
sense of the preciousness of human life. According to St Thomas, human beings are meant to reverence one another out of
reverence for God, in other words, because they can find in
every human being 'something divine' to admire—'the good of
grace or virtue, or of the natural image of God'.[72] To diminish
reverence for God is to shake the foundations of reverence for
man. 'By living "as if God did not exist",' says the century's
greatest Christian interpreter of atheism, 'man loses sight not
only of the mystery of God but also of the mystery of the world
and the mystery of his own being.'[73] To this judgment we can
add another: when Holy Mass is celebrated as if it were not the
awful Sacrifice of the God-Man but no more than an average
entertainment, priests and people grow blind not only to the
mystery of God but to the mystery—and the dignity—of their

[71] *Sacrosanctum concilium*, no. 116.
[72] ST 2a2ae 19, 3, ad 1.
[73] John Paul II, Encyclical letter, *Evangelium vitae*, no. 22.

own humanity. If 'anything goes' at the altar, then anything goes anywhere.

Conclusion—Home to Rome

Where is all this leading? To Rome, of course. Where but to Rome do all roads lead? Rome, the city of the martyrs, of Peter and Paul, of Lawrence and Sixtus. As a Catholic, I cannot speak of pastoral theology without speaking of him who, by the will of the Good Shepherd Himself, pastures the flock of God. Pastoral theology is inevitably Petrine theology.

The theology of beauty—the sensible beauty of Christian art and the spiritual beauty of the saints—has to be Petrine theology. During the age of Iconoclasm, the Popes were the great defenders of the holy beauty of the icons, just as, in the age of Fra Angelico, they were the patrons of the iconographers. And it is also the Popes who officially deploy the Church's discernment of the beauty of holiness: they beatify and canonize. The present Successor of Peter has made these two causes central to his pontificate. He has canonized more saints than any of his predecessors, because he wants to give Christ's faithful as many models as possible to encourage them in the pursuit of holiness. And also, from the beginning, he has championed the renewal of Christian culture and the arts. In 1994, the Holy Father explained how faith and contemplation of Christ can inspire man's cultural endeavours:

> This marvellous creation of man can only flow from the contemplation of Christ's mystery and from listening to His word, put into practice with total sincerity and unreserved commitment, following the example of the Virgin Mary. Faith frees thought and opens new horizons to the language of poetry and the literary arts, to philosophy, to theology, as well as to other forms of creativity proper to the human genius.[74]

---

[74] Address of March 18, 1994.

The Holy Father has presented a further argument. There can be no true culture, no authentic beauty, where *the family* is undermined, where marriage and the procreation of children are despised. The family is the basic cell of human society and therefore of human culture. The Holy Father developed this point in his *Letter to Families* written for the International Year of the Family in 1994. Through the family, he said, human culture becomes a 'civilization of love'. The family is the source of a love that has a true spiritual beauty, 'fairest love':

> When we speak about 'fairest love', we are also speaking about *beauty*: the beauty of love and the beauty of the human being who, by the power of the Holy Spirit, is capable of such love. We are speaking of the beauty of man and woman: their beauty as brother or sister, as a couple about to be married, as husband and wife. The Gospel sheds light not only on the mystery of 'fairest love', but also on the equally profound mystery of beauty, which, like love, is from God. Man and woman are from God, two persons called to become a mutual gift. From the primordial gift of the Spirit, the 'giver of life', there arises the reciprocal gift of being husband and wife, no less than that of being brother or sister.[75]

In the same letter, the Pope speaks of the Incarnation, which gave a new dignity and direction not only to the family but also to the world's art. The Son of God, conceived by the Holy Spirit in the Virgin's womb, chose to be born into a human family, the Holy Family of Nazareth, thus raising every human family to a new and immeasurable grandeur. At the same time, when the Word was made flesh, He became 'the source of a new beauty in the history of humanity'.

> After the strict prohibition against portraying the invisible God by graven images (cf. Dt 4:15–20), the Christian era began instead to portray in art the God who became man, Mary His Mother, St Joseph, the saints of the Old and New Covenant and the entire created world redeemed by Christ.[76]

[75] John Paul II, *Letter to Families*, no. 20.
[76] Ibid.

The two effects of the Incarnation are closely connected. The Holy Family has inspired countless masterpieces of art, which in turn have inspired countless Christian families to a more whole-hearted imitation of Jesus, Mary, and Joseph. The holy beauty has transmitted the beautiful holiness. Thus family and culture are inseparable.

> The Church is conscious that her presence in the contemporary world, and in particular the contribution and support she offers to the promotion of the dignity of marriage and the family, are intimately linked to the development of culture.[77]

Our Western society, says the Pope, is 'a society which is sick'. It is depriving itself of its capacity to fashion beauty. A culture that attacks the family and innocent human life, a culture that prizes sterility and death, has cut itself from the very wellsprings of art. It will generate images only of brutal ugliness, the fatal symptom of its attack on the truth of man.

These are dangerous, countercultural words. They strike at the complacent wisdom of the world, with its adulation of the unnatural and its contempt for the pure. But they are the words of a man who holds the highest martyrological office in the Church. Every Christian is called to bear witness to Christ according to his state of life, but the Pope, *ex officio*, as Vicar of Christ and Successor of Peter, is called to expose himself above all others to the mockery of the world and the fury of its prince. He feeds the sheep, but he must also be ready to lay down his life for them, to stretch forth his hands and be girded and led whither he would not.

The Pope's office is martyrological because it is Christological. In him, as Pope St Leo the Great said, Peter's confession resounds through the universal Church: 'You are the Christ, the Son of the living God.' He bears witness to the Lord Jesus, the incarnate Second Person of the Blessed Trinity, true God and

---

[77] Ibid.

true man in one person, the divine Redeemer of the human race. This Pope, our present Holy Father, John Paul II, bears witness in a special way to the beauty of the Word incarnate. From the beginning, his Christocentricity has been a theological aesthetic. To believe, he says, is to 'let oneself be enchanted by the luminous figure of Jesus the Revealer and by the love of Him who sent Him'.[78] Like Fra Angelico, he asks us to look at Christ shining in the Communion of Saints, the Burning Babe in the Virgin's arms. Here, he says, in this Child, is the key, David's Key, to the renewal of human culture. Look at Jesus living in Mary, and then you will know that there can be no civilization of love that is not a culture of life. God for us became a child; do not, like Herod, try to kill Him in the least and littlest of His brethren. Paul said that Christ is 'made unto us wisdom and justice and sanctification and redemption' (1 Cor 1:30). And, through John Paul II, Peter says: the Lord Jesus is the beauty of holiness, and only from His Heart does holy beauty shine upon the earth.

---

[78] Cited in John Saward, *Christ Is the Answer: The Christ-Centred Teaching of Pope John Paul II* (Edinburgh, 1995), 11.

ART CREDITS

INDEX

Adam, 53–54
Akathaist Hymn, 135
Albert the Great, St
  on beauty, 43–44, 58 n. 135, 61
  on saints, 32, 128, 164–65
  theological aesthetic of the
    Eucharist, 107–8
Ambrose, St, 64, 67
angels, 32–36
Antoninus Pierozzi, St
  Archbishop of Florence, 28
  importance of, 30–31
  on Mary, 126, 129–30, 139, 140
  as patron of Fra Angelico, 69
  and scripture, 39
Apology to Abbot William (Bernard
  of Clairvaux), 109–10
Aristotle, 84, 97
art
  and prudence, 80–81, 109
  religious, 78
  sacred, 77–78, 110–11
artists, 71–73, 80–81
Ascent of Mount Carmel, The (John
  of the Cross), 109–10
Aston, Margaret, 183–84
atheism, 76, 79, 145–46
Augustine, St
  Christ as 'Art' and, 88–89
  on *cupiditas,* 174
  end of the world in, 68 n. 182
  man as image of God, 53
  on martyrs, 161, 176, 179, 180–
    81
  in Mary, 124, 138

and pride, 146
resurrection of the body in, 65
  n. 163, 66–67
aureole in art, 67

Ballad of the White Horse (G. K.
  Chesterton), 181
Ballade of Our Lady (François
  Villon), 157
Balthasar, Hans Urs von
  and beauty, 25
  on Chateaubriand, 22 n .8
  humility in, 109, 147
  on martyrs, 177–78, 181
  on Mary, 114 n. 4, 147, 150
  metaphysics of St Thomas and,
    47
  religion and art in, 76, 90
  and a theological aesthetic, 22
  and theology separated from
    sanctity, 24
  tragedy and comedy, 182
beauty, definitions of, 43–47
Béguin, Albert, 173
Bernanos, Georges, 173–74
  Diary of a Country Priest, 136–37
Bernard of Clairvaux, St
  Apology to Abbot William, 109–10
  on the Incarnation, 37–38, 55
  on Mary, 119 n. 18, 134
Bernard of Morlais, 175
Biscop, Saint Benet, 20
Blake, William, 79
Blount, Charles, 169
Bloy, Léon, 120 n. 20